Python Benchmarking

Measure The Execution Time Of Python Code With time And timeit

Jason Brownlee

2023

Praise for *SuperFast*Python

> *"I'm reading this article now, and it is really well made (simple, concise but comprehensive). Thank you for the effort! Tech industry is going forward thanks also by people like you that diffuse knowledge."*

– **Gabriele Berselli**, Python Developer.

> *"I enjoy your postings and intuitive writeups - keep up the good work"*

– **Martin Gay**, Quantitative Developer at Lacima Group.

> *"Great work. I always enjoy reading your knowledge based articles"*

– **Janath Manohararaj**, Director of Engineering.

> *"Great as always!!!"*

– **Jadranko Belusic**, Software Developer at Crossvallia.

> *"Thank you for sharing your knowledge. Your tutorials are one of the best I've read in years. Unfortunately, most authors, try to prove how clever they are and fail to educate. Yours are very much different. I love the simplicity of the examples on which more complex scenarios can be built on, but, the most important aspect in my opinion, they are easy to understand. Thank you again for all the time and effort spent on creating these tutorials."*

– **Marius Rusu**, Python Developer.

> *"Thanks for putting out excellent content Jason Brownlee, tis much appreciated"*

– **Bilal B.**, Senior Data Engineer.

> *"Thank you for sharing. I've learnt a lot from your tutorials, and, I am still doing, thank you so much again. I wish you all the best."*

– **Sehaba Amine**, Research Intern at LIRIS.

"Wish I had this tutorial 7 yrs ago when I did my first multithreading software. Awesome Jason"

– **Leon Marusa**, Big Data Solutions Project Leader at Elektro Celje.

"This is awesome"

– **Subhayan Ghosh**, Azure Data Engineer at Mercedes-Benz R&D.

Copyright

Disclaimer

Preface

Python concurrency is deeply misunderstood.

Opinions vary from *"Python does not support concurrency"* to *"Python concurrency is buggy"*.

I created the website SuperFastPython.com to directly counter these misunderstandings.

Sometimes Python code can be slow. But how slow is it? How do we know the code is faster after we make changes?

The answer to these questions is benchmarking.

We must benchmark our code in order to discover:

- Exactly how long code takes to execute.
- Exactly how much faster our changed code runs.

It is only with precise and reliable measures of execution time that we can then explore questions about whether code is too slow and whether changes make code faster or not.

Benchmarking big topic and there are many ways we could measure the execution speed of code.

A big problem is that most advice on how to benchmark Python code using outdated APIs like the `time.time()` function or recommendations to always use the modern `timeit` module, which is not always the best approach.

Thankfully, reliable and robust APIs for benchmarking Python code are included in the Python standard API that we can use directly to benchmark statements, snippets, functions, and entire programs.

I wrote this book to show you how.

Together, we can make Python code run faster.

Thank you for letting me guide you along this path.

Jason Brownlee, Ph.D.
2023.

Contents

II   Benchmarking With `time`   25

V Benchmarking Asyncio   219

Part I

Benchmarking Background

Chapter 1

Introduction

Welcome to *Python Benchmarking*!

Python code can be slow.

We can benchmark Python code discover exactly how slow it is, then test changes to the code to confirm that the changes we made had the desired effect.

Benchmarking is required to develop fast programs.

This book teaches you how to benchmark the execution time of Python code.

It is not a dry, long-winded academic textbook. Instead, it is a crash course for Python developers that provides carefully designed tutorials with complete and working code examples that you can copy-paste into your project today and get results.

Before we dive into the tutorials, let's look at what is coming with a breakdown of this book.

1.1 Who Is This For

Before we dive in, let's make sure you're in the right place.

This book is designed for Python developers who want to discover how to benchmark Python code.

Specifically, this book is for:

- Developers that can write simple Python programs.
- Developers that need better performance from current or future Python programs.

This book does not require that you are an expert in the Python programming language, profiling, or benchmarking.

Specifically:

- You do not need to be an expert Python developer.
- You do not need to be an expert in code benchmarking.
- You do not need to be an expert at performance optimization.

Next, let's take a look at what this book will cover.

1.2 Book Overview

This book is designed to bring you up-to-speed with benchmarking as fast as possible.

As such, it is not exhaustive. There are many topics that are interesting or helpful but are not on the critical path to getting you productive fast.

This book is divided into 7 parts, they are:

- **Part I: Background**. Tutorials on getting up to speed with code benchmarking.
- **Part II: Benchmarking With `time`**. Tutorials on how to benchmark using functions in the `time` module.
- **Part III: Benchmarking Best Practices**. Tutorials on the best practices and tips to consider when benchmarking code.
- **Part IV: Benchmarking Helpers**. Tutorials on how to develop helper functions and objects to make benchmarking simpler.

- **Part V: Benchmarking Asyncio**. Tutorials on how to benchmark coroutines and asyncio programs.
- **Part VI: Benchmarking With `timeit`**. Tutorials on how to benchmark using the `timeit` module.
- **Part VII: Other Benchmarking**. Tutorials on related techniques such as profiling and command line tools.

The book is further divided into 25 tutorials across the four parts, they are:

Part I: Background:

- **Tutorial 01**: Introduction.
- **Tutorial 02**: Benchmarking Python.

Part II: Benchmarking With `time`:

- **Tutorial 03**: Benchmarking With `time.time()`
- **Tutorial 04**: Benchmarking With `time.monotonic()`
- **Tutorial 05**: Benchmarking With `time.perf_counter()`
- **Tutorial 06**: Benchmarking With `time.thread_time()`
- **Tutorial 07**: Benchmarking With `time.process_time()`
- **Tutorial 08**: Comparing `time` Module Functions

Part III: Benchmarking Best Practices:

- **Tutorial 09**: Benchmark Metrics
- **Tutorial 10**: Benchmark Repetition
- **Tutorial 11**: Benchmark Reporting

Part IV: Benchmarking Helpers:

- **Tutorial 12**: Benchmark Helper Function
- **Tutorial 13**: Benchmark Stopwatch Class
- **Tutorial 14**: Benchmark Context Manager
- **Tutorial 15**: Benchmark Function Decorator

Part V: Benchmarking Asyncio:

- **Tutorial 16**: Gentle Introduction to Asyncio
- **Tutorial 17**: Benchmarking Asyncio With `loop.time()`
- **Tutorial 18**: Benchmark Helper Coroutine

- **Tutorial 19**: Benchmark Asynchronous Context Manager
- **Tutorial 20**: Benchmark Coroutine Decorator

Part VI: Benchmarking With `timeit`:

- **Tutorial 21**: Benchmarking With The `timeit` Module
- **Tutorial 22**: Benchmarking With `timeit.timeit()`
- **Tutorial 23**: Benchmarking With The `timeit` Command Line

Part VII: Other Benchmarking:

- **Tutorial 24**: Profile Python Code
- **Tutorial 25**: Benchmarking With The `time` Command

Next, let's take a closer look at how the tutorials are structured.

1.3   Tutorial Structure

This book teaches Python benchmarking by example.

Each lesson has a specific learning outcome and is designed to be completed in less than one hour.

Each lesson is also designed to be self-contained so that you can read the lessons out of order if you choose, such as dipping into topics in the future to solve specific programming problems.

The lessons were written with some intentional repetition of key APIs and concepts. These gentle reminders are designed to help embed the common usage patterns in your mind so that they become second nature.

We Python developers learn best from real and working code examples.

Next, let's learn more about the code examples provided in this book.

1.4   Code Examples

All code examples use Python 3.

Python 2.7 is not supported because it reached its end of life in 2020.

I recommend using the most recent version of Python 3 available at the time you are reading this, although Python 3.11 or higher is sufficient to run all code examples in this book.

You do not require any specific integrated development environment (IDE). I recommend typing code into a simple text editor like Sublime Text that runs on all modern operating systems. I'm a Sublime user myself, but any text editor will do. If you are familiar with an IDE, then, by all means, use it.

Each code example is complete and can be run as a standalone program. I recommend running code examples from the command line (also called the command prompt on Windows or terminal on macOS) to avoid any possible issues.

The procedure to run a Python program from the command line is as follows:

1. Save the code file to a directory of your choice with a `.py` extension.
2. Open your command line.
3. Change the directory to the location where you saved the Python program.
4. Execute the program using the Python interpreter followed by the name of the program.

For example:

```
python my_program.py
```

I recommend running programs on the command line. It is easy, it works for everyone, it avoids all kinds of problems that beginners have with notebooks and IDEs, and programs run fastest on the command line.

That being said, if you know what you're doing, you can run code examples within your IDE or a notebook if you like. Editors like Sublime Text will let you run Python programs directly, and this is fine. I just can't help you debug any issues you might encounter because they're probably caused by your development environment.

Most tutorials in this book provide code examples. These are typically introduced first via snippets of code that begin with an ellipsis (. . .) to clearly indicate that they are not a complete code example. After the program is introduced via snippets, a complete code example is listed that includes all of the snippets tied together, with any additional glue code and import statements.

I recommend typing code examples from scratch to help you learn and memorize the APIs.

Beware of copy-pasting code from the EBook version of this book as you may accidentally lose or add white space, which may break the execution of the program.

A code file is provided for each complete example in the book organized by tutorial and example within each tutorial. You can execute these programs directly or use them as a reference.

You can download all code examples from here:

- Download Code Examples.
  https://superfastpython.com/pb-code

All code examples were tested on a POSIX machine by myself and my technical editors prior to publication.

APIs can change over time, functions can become deprecated, and idioms can change and be replaced. I keep this book up to date with changes to the Python standard library and you can email me any time to get the latest version. Nevertheless, if you encounter any warnings or problems with the code, please contact me immediately and I will fix them. I pride myself on having complete and working code examples in all of my tutorials.

Next, let's consider the benchmark results reported in this book.

1.5   Benchmark Results

This book is generally interested in teaching benchmarking with code examples.

Therefore, many of the tutorials will involve benchmarking execution time, e.g. wall clock time and comparing results.

All benchmark results were recorded on a test workstation. The benchmark workstation was an i7 iMac with 4 physical CPU cores and 8 logical CPU cores with hyperthreading. Python 3.11.4 was used. You don't need to match this version number.

Expect benchmark results to differ on your system. Take the listed execution times qualitatively, rather than absolute scores. They are directional, showing a trend of better performance. You are expected to see similar trends when executing the code examples on your own system, although with different specific numbers.

The execution time of each program will vary each time an example is run. This is due to the natural variation on the system, caused by whatever else the operating system decided to do at the same time. We will explicitly address this in the best practices section of the book.

Next, let's consider how we might approach working through this book.

1.6   How To Read

You can work at your own pace.

There's no rush and I recommend that you take your time.

This book is designed to be read linearly from start to finish, guiding you from being a Python developer at the start of the book to being a Python developer that can confidently benchmark Python code by the end of the book.

In order to avoid overload, I recommend completing one or two tutorials per day, such as in the evening or during your lunch break. This will allow you to complete the transformation in about one month.

I recommend maintaining a directory with all of the code you type from the tutorials in the book. This will allow you to use the directory as your own private code library, allowing you to copy-paste code into your projects in the future.

I recommend trying to adapt and extend the examples in the tutorials. Play with them. Break them. This will help you learn more about how the API works and why we follow specific usage patterns.

Next, let's review your newfound capabilities after completing this book.

1.7 Learning Outcomes

This book will transform you into a Python developer that can benchmark Python code on your projects.

1. You will confidently use functions from the `time` module for benchmarking, including:

1. How to benchmark statements, functions, and programs using the 5 functions for measuring time in the `time` module.
2. How to know when and why to use functions like `time.perf_counter()` and `time.monotonic()` over `time.time()`.
3. How to know when and why to use functions like `time.thread_time()` and `time.process_time()`.

2. You will confidently know benchmarking best practices and when to use them, including:

1. How to calculate and report benchmark results in terms of difference and speedup.
2. How to and why to repeat benchmark tests and report summary statistics like the average.

3. How to consider the precision and units of measure of reported benchmark results.

3. You will confidently develop convenient benchmarking tools, including:

1. How to develop a custom benchmarking helper function and stopwatch class.
2. How to develop a custom benchmarking context manager.
3. How to develop a custom benchmarking function decorator.

4. You will confidently know how to benchmark asyncio programs and develop convenient async-specific benchmarking tools, including:

1. How to benchmark asyncio programs using the event loop timer.
2. How to develop a custom benchmarking coroutine.
3. How to develop a custom benchmarking asynchronous context manager and coroutine decorator.

5. You will confidently know how to benchmark snippets using the `timeit` module, including:

1. How to benchmark statements and functions using the `timeit` Python API.
2. How to benchmark snippets of code using the `timeit` command line interface.

6. You will confidently know how to use other benchmarking tools, including:

1. How to profile Python programs with the built-in profiler and know the relationship between benchmarking and profiling.
2. How to benchmark the execution time of Python programs unobtrusively using the `time` Unix command.

Next, let's discover how we can get help when working through the book.

1.8   Getting Help

The tutorials in this book were designed to be easy to read and follow.

Nevertheless, sometimes we need a little extra help.

A list of further reading resources is provided at the end of each tutorial. These can be helpful if you are interested in learning more about the topic covered, such as fine-grained details of the standard library and API functions used.

The conclusions at the end of the book provide a complete list of websites and books that can help if you want to learn more about Python benchmarking and the relevant parts of the Python standard library. It also lists places where you can go online and ask questions about Python.

Finally, if you ever have questions about the tutorials or code in this book, you can contact me any time and I will do my best to help. My contact details are provided at the end of the book.

Now that we know what's coming, let's get started.

1.8.1   Next

Next up in the first tutorial, we will look at the importance of benchmarking execution time.

Chapter 2

Benchmarking Python

Benchmarking execution time is required to improve the performance of code.

Code performance is a critical aspect of modern software development. Modern projects have performance requirements as part of the project from the beginning, ensuring responses are timely and user experience is consistent.

Therefore we cannot neglect performance benchmarking and the most common type of performance benchmarking which is benchmarking execution time.

In this tutorial, you will discover benchmarking Python code and the importance of benchmarking execution time.

After completing this tutorial, you will know:

- What is code benchmarking and the 3 primary aspects of benchmarking.
- What are the different types of benchmarking and the importance of benchmarking execution time.
- What are the key considerations when benchmarking and how benchmarking is different from profiling.

Let's get started.

2.1   What Is Benchmarking

Benchmarking is critical if we care about the performance of our Python code.

Benchmarking is a systematic and methodical process of evaluating the performance of software by measuring how it executes specific tasks or processes.

> Benchmarking is the practice of comparing business processes and performance metrics to industry bests and best practices from other companies. Dimensions typically measured are quality, time and cost.

– Benchmarking, Wikipedia.

It's a practice that allows us to gain a precise understanding of how long code takes to run, how much memory it consumes, and how efficiently it uses available system resources.

Benchmarking also provides insights that empower us to optimize our code, make informed decisions about resource allocation, and ensure software quality.

At its core, code benchmarking involves executing specific code segments or entire programs while carefully measuring key performance metrics. These metrics can include execution time, memory usage, throughput, latency, and more, depending on the specific goals of the benchmark.

By collecting and analyzing this data, we can identify bottlenecks, regressions, and areas for improvement, leading to more efficient, responsive, and cost-effective software solutions.

But benchmarking isn't just about running code and recording numbers; it's a multifaceted process that demands controlled testing conditions, careful interpretation of results, and a deep understanding of the specific requirements of our project.

Next, let's consider the three main aspects of benchmarking code.

2.2   3 Aspects Of Benchmarking

Benchmarking code involves many concerns to ensure accurate and meaningful performance measurements.

Nevertheless, the three primary aspects of benchmarking code are:

1. Measurement and metrics.
2. Controlled testing conditions.
3. Interpretation and analysis.

Let's take a closer look at each in turn.

2.2.1   Measurement And Metrics

This aspect involves defining what we want to measure and selecting the appropriate performance metrics.

Common metrics include execution time, memory usage, throughput, latency, and resource utilization.

Deciding which metrics are relevant to our specific use case is a crucial step.

2.2.2   Controlled Testing Conditions

To obtain reliable and consistent benchmark results, we need to establish controlled testing conditions.

This includes isolating the code to be benchmarked from external factors, minimizing interference from background processes, and ensuring that the system is in a stable state during testing.

Reproducibility is key, meaning that the same benchmark should yield consistent results when run multiple times.

2.2.3   Interpretation And Analysis

Benchmarking is not just about collecting data; it also involves interpreting and analyzing the results.

This includes comparing benchmark results, identifying performance bottlenecks, and making informed decisions about optimizations or resource allocation.

Effective analysis is essential for drawing meaningful insights from the benchmark data.

Next, let's consider some common types of benchmarking.

2.3   Types Of Benchmarking

Benchmarking code can take various forms, depending on what we want to measure and evaluate.

Five main types of code benchmarking include:

1. **Execution Time Benchmarking**: This type of benchmarking measures the time it takes for a specific piece of code to execute. It's one of the most common forms of benchmarking and is used to evaluate the performance of algorithms, functions, or entire programs.
2. **Memory Usage Benchmarking**: Memory benchmarking assesses the amount of system memory (RAM) consumed by a program or specific code segment. It's essential for identifying memory leaks or inefficient memory management.
3. **Throughput Benchmarking**: Throughput benchmarking evaluates the rate at which a system or component can process a certain volume of data or requests within a given time frame. This is commonly used in networking and server performance assessment.
4. **Latency Benchmarking**: Latency benchmarking measures the time it takes for a system to respond to a specific event or request. It's crucial for assessing the responsiveness of real-time systems, such as web applications and communication protocols.
5. **Scalability Benchmarking**: Scalability benchmarking focuses on how a system or application performs as the workload or input size increases. It helps identify the limits of a system's

scalability and can guide decisions related to resource allocation and architecture design.

Each type of benchmarking serves a specific purpose in performance evaluation and optimization.

Depending on the goals of our analysis, we may choose one or more of these benchmarking types to measure and assess different aspects of our code or system's performance.

Next, let's take a closer look at benchmarking the execution time of code.

2.4 Why Benchmark Execution Time

Benchmarking code execution time is a fundamental practice for delivering efficient and responsive software applications.

The main reason we benchmark execution time is to improve performance.

- **Performance Optimization**: Benchmarking helps identify performance bottlenecks and areas where code execution can be optimized. By measuring and analyzing execution times, we can focus optimization efforts on the most critical sections of code.

We measure the performance so that we can improve it.

This typically involves a baseline measurement, then a measurement of performance after each change to confirm the change moved performance in the right direction.

Other reasons we may want to benchmark execution time include:

1. **Requirements**: Code that meets performance requirements is essential for a positive user experience. Benchmarking ensures that software performs efficiently and consistently under various conditions, contributing to high-quality applications.
2. **Regressions**: Benchmarking is a valuable tool for detecting performance regressions. When new code changes are intro-

duced, benchmarking can help identify whether performance has improved or deteriorated, allowing developers to address regressions promptly.

Benchmarking execution time is also the foundation of other types of benchmarking, such as latency, throughput, and scalability benchmarking.

Next, let's consider the consequences of not taking performance benchmarking seriously in our Python projects.

2.4.1   Consequences Of Ignoring Execution Time

Neglecting the benchmarking of code execution time can have several significant consequences, which can impact both the development process and the quality of the software being developed.

Some of the key consequences include:

1. **Performance Issues**: Without proper benchmarking, we may inadvertently release software that performs poorly. This can lead to user dissatisfaction, slow response times, and a negative user experience.
2. **Resource Inefficiency**: Unoptimized code can consume unnecessary system resources, such as excessive CPU usage or memory usage. This inefficiency can result in higher operational costs and resource contention with other applications.
3. **Scalability Problems**: Neglecting benchmarking may lead to a lack of understanding about how the software scales with increased workloads. As a result, the software may not be able to handle growing user demands effectively.
4. **Poor User Experience**: Sluggish and unresponsive software can frustrate users and drive them away. This can have negative implications for user retention and customer satisfaction.
5. **Long-Term Costs**: Ignoring benchmarking can lead to long-term costs associated with fixing performance issues, scaling the system, and addressing user complaints. Early performance optimization is often more cost-effective.

To avoid these consequences, it's crucial to take code benchmarking seriously as an integral part of the software development process.

Next, let's consider some common considerations when benchmarking the execution time of code.

2.4.2 Considerations When Benchmarking Execution Time

When benchmarking execution time and optimizing the performance of code, several common concerns and challenges may arise.

These concerns should be carefully addressed to ensure accurate and effective performance analysis.

Some of the key concerns include:

1. Careful consideration of what code is being benchmarked.

1. **Real-World Scenarios**: Benchmarking in realistic scenarios is vital. Synthetic benchmarks may not reflect real-world usage patterns, so tests should mimic actual user interactions or system workloads.
2. **Resource Contention**: Resource contention, such as competition for CPU, memory, or I/O resources, can affect benchmark results. Isolating code and minimizing resource contention is important for accurate measurements.
3. **Micro-Optimizations**: Focusing on micro-optimizations (small, low-impact changes) without addressing fundamental issues can lead to suboptimal performance. It's important to prioritize high-impact optimizations and algorithmic improvements.

2. Careful consideration of how code is being benchmarked.

1. **Benchmarking Environment**: Variations in the benchmarking environment, such as hardware configurations, operating systems, and system loads, can introduce inconsistencies in performance measurements. It's essential to control and document

the benchmarking environment to make results reproducible
and reliable.
2. **Benchmarking Tools**: Selecting appropriate benchmarking
   tools and methodologies is critical. Using dedicated tools,
   custom tools, or benchmarking libraries can ensure consistent
   and reliable measurements.
3. **Warm-Up Time**: Code may require a warm-up period before
   reaching peak performance. Ignoring the warm-up time can
   lead to inaccurate measurements, as the initial runs may not
   reflect the code's optimized behavior.

3. Careful consideration of measurements used in the benchmark.

1. **Measurement Precision**: The precision of timers and measurement tools can impact the accuracy of benchmark results.
   Using the most appropriate timing functions with sufficient
   precision and resolution is crucial to minimize measurement
   errors.
2. **Statistical Variability**: Performance measurements can ex-
   hibit statistical variability due to various factors, including
   background processes and random fluctuations. To mitigate
   this, it's important to conduct multiple benchmark runs and
   report averages.
3. **Sample Size**: The number of benchmark runs can affect result
   reliability. A small sample size may not provide a representative
   picture of code performance, while a large sample size can
   increase the accuracy of results.

Addressing these concerns and adhering to best practices in benchmarking and performance optimization helps ensure that code performs optimally and meets user expectations for responsiveness and
efficiency.

Next let's contrast benchmarking execution time to code profiling.

2.5 Benchmarking Vs. Code Profiling

Benchmarking the execution time of code is a different task from code profiling.

They are both essential techniques for code performance analysis and optimization, but they serve slightly different purposes and employ distinct methodologies.

Let's, compare and contrast these two approaches:

2.5.1 Benchmarking Execution Time

Benchmarking execution time primarily aims to measure how long it takes for a piece of code or an application to perform a specific task.

The primary goal is to quantify the speed and efficiency of code execution.

It provides an overall assessment of code performance, emphasizing metrics like a time measure. Benchmarking typically assesses the entire program or specific functions in isolation.

Benchmarking often involves comparing different implementations or versions of code to determine which one performs better. It helps in selecting the most efficient solution for a given task, or whether candidate solutions improve the performance of a task.

2.5.2 Code Profiling

Code profiling focuses on understanding how code behaves internally. It identifies which parts of the code consume the most resources and may uncover performance bottlenecks.

It offers a detailed examination of code execution. It identifies specific functions, methods, or lines of code that may be causing performance issues.

Profiling tools can provide data at a very granular level, showing details like function call counts, time spent in specific functions, and memory usage. This level of detail is often valuable for pinpointing issues.

Profiling is commonly used as a diagnostic tool to discover areas for code optimization. It helps developers focus on specific code segments that need improvement.

2.5.3 Comparison

Now that we are familiar with both benchmarking and profiling, let's compare them.

1. **Complementary Tools**: Benchmarking and profiling are often used together. Profiling helps identify performance bottlenecks, and benchmarking verifies whether optimizations have the desired impact on execution time.
2. **Level of Detail**: Benchmarking provides a high-level overview of performance, while profiling offers a deep dive into the internals of the code. The choice depends on the specific goal of the analysis.
3. **Optimization Focus**: Benchmarking is more focused on comparing different implementations or versions, while profiling is about fine-tuning and optimizing existing code.
4. **Scope**: Benchmarking tends to assess a system as a whole or specific function in isolation, whereas profiling can pinpoint performance issues down to the line of code or instruction.

Benchmarking execution time and code profiling are valuable tools for assessing and enhancing code performance.

While they share a common goal of optimization, they differ in their focus and the level of detail they provide.

Benchmarking is well-suited for comparative performance evaluations, while profiling is indispensable for diagnosing and optimizing code at a fine-grained level.

These approaches are often used in tandem to achieve well-rounded performance improvements in software development. For example, while benchmarking, we may profile code in order to identify parts of

the code to change, propose changes, and benchmark the new version
to confirm the change had the desired impact on performance.

2.6   Further Reading

This section lists helpful additional resources on the topic.

- Benchmarking, Wikipedia.
  https://en.wikipedia.org/wiki/Benchmarking

2.7   Takeaways

You now know about the importance of benchmarking code generally
and code execution time.

Specifically, you know:

- What is code benchmarking and the 3 primary aspects of
  benchmarking.
- What are the different types of benchmarking and the importance of benchmarking execution time.
- What are the key considerations when benchmarking and how
  benchmarking is different from profiling.

2.7.1   Next

In the next tutorial, we will explore benchmarking with the `time`
module.

Part II

Benchmarking With time

The `time` module provides functions for working with clocks and time.

There are five main ways to retrieve the current time using `time` module, they are:

1. Use `time.time()`
2. Use `time.perf_counter()`
3. Use `time.monotonic()`
4. Use `time.process_time()`
5. Use `time.thread_time()`

Each of these functions returns a time in seconds, and each function has an equivalent function that returns the time in nanoseconds. Nevertheless, we will focus our attention on the versions of the function that return time in seconds.

Each function has different qualities and most use different underlying clocks.

All can be used for benchmarking Python code, most are, although perhaps only a few should be used in most circumstances.

The chapters that follow show how to use each time function for benchmarking in turn, followed by a comparison of the functions.

Chapter 3

Benchmarking With `time.time()`

You can benchmark Python code using the `time.time()` function.

In this tutorial, you will discover how to benchmark Python code using the `time.time()` function.

After completing this tutorial, you will know:

- What is the `time.time()` function and its limitations when used for benchmarking.
- How to check the properties of the `time.time()` function such as whether it is adjustable and monotonic.
- How to use the `time.time()` function to benchmark statements, functions, and programs.

Let's get started.

3.1 What Is `time.time()`

The `time.time()` function returns the number of seconds since the epoch.

> Return the time in seconds since the epoch as a floating

point number.

– `time` – Time access and conversions

Recall that the epoch is January 1st 1970, which is used on Unix systems and beyond as an arbitrary fixed time in the past.

> In computing, an epoch is a fixed date and time used as a reference from which a computer measures system time. Most computer systems determine time as a number representing the seconds removed from a particular arbitrary date and time. For instance, Unix and POSIX measure time as the number of seconds that have passed since Thursday 1 January 1970 00:00:00 UT, a point in time known as the Unix epoch.

– Epoch (computing), Wikipedia.

Because the `time.time()` function is based on the system clock, it means that the times returned may change, sometimes quite dramatically. This is referred to the clock used by `time.time()` as being adjustable.

This change can occur for many reasons, such as the user changing the clock time, the clock being updated because of a leap second, or the clock changing due to synchronizing with a time server.

The return value is a floating point value, potentially offering fractions of a second.

The `time.time()` function is not perfect.

It is possible for a subsequent call to `time.time()` to return a value in seconds less than the previous value. This means that the times returned from the function are not monotonic.

> Note that even though the time is always returned as a floating point number, not all systems provide time with a better precision than 1 second. While this function normally returns non-decreasing values, it can return a lower value than a previous call if the system clock has been set back between the two calls.

– `time` – Time access and conversions

This may make the `time.time()` method of benchmarking code appropriate for code that has a generally longer execution time (e.g. seconds) rather than short execution times, e.g. less than a second or less than 500 milliseconds.

The `time.time()` function is widely used for benchmarking in Python, although other more reliable functions should be used instead. We will explore these issues in a later chapter. For now, we will just look at how to use the function for benchmarking.

Now that we know about the `time.time()` function, let's look at how we can use it to benchmark code.

3.2 How To Benchmark

We can use the `time.time()` function to benchmark code.

There are perhaps 3 case studies we may want to consider, they are:

1. Benchmarking a statement.
2. Benchmarking a function.
3. Benchmarking a program.

Let's look at how we can benchmark with the `time.time()` function.

3.2.1 How To Benchmark A Statement

We can use the `time.time()` function to benchmark arbitrary statements.

The procedure is as follows:

1. Record `time.time()` before the statement.
2. Execute the statement.
3. Record `time.time()` after the statement.
4. Subtract start time from after time to give duration.
5. Report the duration using `print()`.

For example:

```
...
# record start time
time_start = time()
# execute the statement
...
# record end time
time_end = time()
# calculate the duration
time_duration = time_end - time_start
# report the duration
print(f'Took {time_duration:.3f} seconds')
```

3.2.2   How To Benchmark A Function

We can use the `time.time()` function to benchmark arbitrary functions.

The procedure is as follows:

1. Record `time.time()` before the function.
2. Call the function.
3. Record `time.time()` after the function.
4. Subtract start time from after time to give duration.
5. Report the duration using `print()`.

For example:

```
...
# record start time
time_start = time()
# call the function
...
# record end time
time_end = time()
# calculate the duration
time_duration = time_end - time_start
# report the duration
print(f'Took {time_duration:.3f} seconds')
```

3.2.3   How To Benchmark A Program

We can use the `time.time()` function to benchmark arbitrary programs (script files).

It requires that the entry point into the program is first moved into a new function, that we will call `main()`. This is to make it easy for all code in the program to be wrapped in the benchmarking code.

The procedure is as follows:

1. Move the entry of the program into a `main()` function (if needed).
2. Record `time.time()` before the `main()` function.
3. Call the `main()` function.
4. Record `time.time()` after the `main()` function.
5. Subtract start time from after time to give duration.
6. Report the duration using `print()`.

For example:

```
# protect the entry point
if __name__ == '__main__':
    # record start time
    time_start = time()
    # execute the program
    main()
    # record end time
    time_end = time()
    # calculate the duration
    time_duration = time_end - time_start
    # report the duration
    print(f'Took {time_duration:.3f} seconds')
```

Now that we know how to benchmark code using `time.time()`, let's look at some worked examples.

3.3   Example Of Benchmarking A Statement

We can explore how to use `time.time()` to benchmark a statement with a worked example.

In this example, we will define a statement that creates a list of 100 million squared integers in a list comprehension, which should take a number of seconds.

```
...
# execute the statement
data = [i*i for i in range(100000000)]
```

We will then surround this statement with benchmarking code.

Firstly, we will record the start time using the `time.time()` function.

```
...
# record start time
time_start = time()
```

Afterward, we will record the end time, calculate the overall execution duration, and report the result.

```
...
# record end time
time_end = time()
# calculate the duration
time_duration = time_end - time_start
# report the duration
print(f'Took {time_duration:.3f} seconds')
```

Tying this together, the complete example is listed below.

```
# SuperFastPython.com
# example of benchmarking a statement with time.time()
from time import time
# record start time
time_start = time()
# execute the statement
data = [i*i for i in range(100000000)]
```

```
# record end time
time_end = time()
# calculate the duration
time_duration = time_end - time_start
# report the duration
print(f'Took {time_duration:.3f} seconds')
```

Running the example first records the start time, the number of seconds since the epoch.

Next, the statement is executed, in this case creating a list of 100 million squared integers.

The end time is then recorded, as the number of seconds since the epoch.

The difference between the two recorded times is calculated, providing the statement execution duration in seconds.

Finally, the result is reported, truncated to three decimal places (milliseconds).

In this case, we can see that the statement took about 5.228 seconds to complete.

Note, the results on your system may differ.

This highlights how we can benchmark a statement using the `time.time()` function.

```
Took 5.228 seconds
```

Next, let's explore an example of benchmarking a function using the `time.time()` function.

3.4   Example Of Benchmarking A Function

We can explore how to use `time.time()` to benchmark a function with a worked example.

In this example, we will define a function that creates a list of 100
million squared integers in a list comprehension, which should take
a number of seconds.

```python
# function to benchmark
def task():
    # create a large list
    data = [i*i for i in range(100000000)]
```

We will then call this function, and surround the function call with
benchmarking code.

Firstly, we will record the start time using the `time.time()` function.

```python
...
# record start time
time_start = time()
```

Afterward, we will record the end time, calculate the overall execution
duration, and report the result.

```python
...
# record end time
time_end = time()
# calculate the duration
time_duration = time_end - time_start
# report the duration
print(f'Took {time_duration:.3f} seconds')
```

Tying this together, the complete example is listed below.

```python
# SuperFastPython.com
# example of benchmarking a function with time.time()
from time import time

# function to benchmark
def task():
    # create a large list
    data = [i*i for i in range(100000000)]

# record start time
```

```
time_start = time()
# execute the function
task()
# record end time
time_end = time()
# calculate the duration
time_duration = time_end - time_start
# report the duration
print(f'Took {time_duration:.3f} seconds')
```

Running the example first records the start time, the number of seconds since the epoch.

Next, the function is called, in this case creating a list of 100 million squared integers.

The end time is then recorded, as the number of seconds since the epoch.

The difference between the two recorded times is calculated, providing the function execution duration in seconds.

Finally, the result is reported, truncated to three decimal places (milliseconds).

In this case, we can see that the function took about 6.220 seconds to complete.

Note, the results on your system may differ.

This highlights how we can benchmark a function using the `time.time()` function.

```
Took 6.220 seconds
```

Next, let's explore an example of benchmarking a program using the `time.time()` function.

3.5 Example Of Benchmarking A Program

We can explore how to use `time.time()` to benchmark a program with a worked example.

In this example, we will update the above example so that it has a `main()` function and protects the entry point, like a more elaborate Python program.

```python
# main function for program
def main():
    # call a function
    task()
```

We will then add benchmarking code around the call to the `main()` function.

```python
# protect the entry point
if __name__ == '__main__':
    # record start time
    time_start = time()
    # execute the program
    main()
    # record end time
    time_end = time()
    # calculate the duration
    time_duration = time_end - time_start
    # report the duration
    print(f'Took {time_duration:.3f} seconds')
```

Tying this together, the complete example is listed below.

```python
# SuperFastPython.com
# example of benchmarking a program with time.time()
from time import time

# function to benchmark
def task():
```

```
    # create a large list
    data = [i*i for i in range(100000000)]

# main function for program
def main():
    # call a function
    task()

# protect the entry point
if __name__ == '__main__':
    # record start time
    time_start = time()
    # execute the program
    main()
    # record end time
    time_end = time()
    # calculate the duration
    time_duration = time_end - time_start
    # report the duration
    print(f'Took {time_duration:.3f} seconds')
```

Running the example first records the start time, the number of seconds since the epoch.

Next, the **main()** function is called which executes the core of the program. In this case, it calls our **task()** function and creates a list of 100 million squared integers.

The end time is then recorded, as the number of seconds since the epoch.

The difference between the two recorded times is calculated, providing the function execution duration in seconds.

Finally, the result is reported, truncated to three decimal places (milliseconds).

In this case, we can see that the function took about 6.341 seconds to complete.

Note, the results on your system may differ.

This highlights how we can benchmark a program using the `time.time()` function.

```
Took 6.341 seconds
```

3.6   Example Of Checking Sleep Time

The `time.time()` function does include time spent blocked or sleeping.

When the program is blocked or sleeping, the clock used by `time.time()` is not paused.

We can demonstrate this with a worked example.

We can update the example of benchmarking a statement and include a sleep for 2 seconds.

For example:

```
...
# sleep for a moment
sleep(2)
```

This will have an effect on the benchmark time, e.g. it should increase the benchmark time from about 5 seconds to about 7 seconds.

Tying this together, the complete example is listed below.

```
# SuperFastPython.com
# example of benchmarking with sleep via time.time()
from time import time
from time import sleep
# record start time
time_start = time()
# execute the statement
data = [i*i for i in range(100000000)]
# sleep for a moment
sleep(2)
```

```
# record end time
time_end = time()
# calculate the duration
time_duration = time_end - time_start
# report the duration
print(f'Took {time_duration:.3f} seconds')
```

Running the example, we can see that the addition of the `sleep()` after the target code does have the intended effect.

The time of the benchmark increases from about 5 seconds to about 7 seconds.

Note, the results on your system may differ.

This highlights that time spent explicitly sleeping is included in the benchmark time when using `time.time()`.

```
Took 7.168 seconds
```

3.7 Example Of Checking Clock Properties

The clock used by the `time.time()` function is adjustable.

This means that the system may change the clock while our program is running, possibly making any benchmark results invalid.

Because the clock can be adjusted, it means that it is not monotonic. This means it is possible for future values of the clock to be less than or before past values, due to updates.

We can confirm this by reporting the details of the `"time"` function in the `time` module via the `time.get_clock_info()` function.

This reports the details of the clock used by a function, such as whether it is adjustable, how it is implemented on the platform, whether it is monotonic, and the resolution on the platform.

The program below reports the details of the clock used by the
time.time() function.

```
# SuperFastPython.com
# details of the clock used by time.time()
from time import get_clock_info
# get details
details = get_clock_info('time')
# report details
print(details)
```

Running the program reports the details of the "time" clock.

We can see that indeed it is not monotonic. We can also confirm
that it is adjustable.

Note, the results on your system may differ.

This highlights how we can check the details of the clock used by a
time function.

```
namespace(
    implementation='clock_gettime(CLOCK_REALTIME)',
    monotonic=False,
    adjustable=True,
    resolution=1.0000000000000002e-06)
```

3.8   Further Reading

This section lists helpful additional resources on the topic.

- Epoch (computing), Wikipedia.
  https://en.wikipedia.org/wiki/Epoch_(computing)
- time – Time access and conversions.
  https://docs.python.org/3/library/time.html

3.9 Takeaways

You now know how to benchmark Python code using the `time.time()` function.

Specifically, you know:

- What is the `time.time()` function and its limitations when used for benchmarking.
- How to check the properties of the `time.time()` function such as whether it is adjustable and monotonic.
- How to use the `time.time()` function to benchmark statements, functions, and programs.

3.9.1 Next

In the next tutorial, we will explore how to benchmark with the `time.monotonic()` function.

Chapter 4

Benchmarking With `time.monotonic()`

You can benchmark Python code using the `time.monotonic()` function.

In this tutorial, you will discover how to benchmark Python code using the `time.monotonic()` function.

After completing this tutorial, you will know:

- What is the `time.monotonic()` function and its strengths and limitations when used for benchmarking.
- How to check the properties of the `time.monotonic()` function such as whether it is adjustable and monotonic.
- How to use the `time.monotonic()` function to benchmark statements, functions, and programs.

Let's get started.

4.1 What Is `time.monotonic()`

The `time.monotonic()` function returns timestamps from a clock that cannot go backwards, as its name suggests.

In mathematics, monotonic, e.g. a monotonic function means a function whose output increases (or decreases).

This means that the result from the `time.monotonic()` function will never be before the result from a prior call.

> Return the value (in fractional seconds) of a monotonic clock, i.e. a clock that cannot go backwards.

– `time` – Time access and conversions.

It is a high-resolution timestamp, although is not relative to epoch-like `time.time()`. Instead, it uses a separate timer separate from the system clock. This means that it is not affected by changes to the system clock, such as updates or clock adjustments due to time synchronization.

It also means that the times returned from the `time.monotonic()` function can be compared to each other, relatively, but not to the system clock.

The `time.monotonic()` function generally has a lower resolution than the `time.perf_counter()` function.

> The clock is not affected by system clock updates. The reference point of the returned value is undefined, so that only the difference between the results of two calls is valid.

– `time` – Time access and conversions.

The `time.monotonic()` function is "system-wide", meaning that different programs or threads in the same program on the same system can access the same underlying clock.

The `time.monotonic()` function was introduced in Python version 3.3 with the intent of addressing the limitations of the `time.time()` function tied to the system clock, such as use in short-duration timing.

> `monotonic()`: Monotonic clock (cannot go backward), not affected by system clock updates.

– What's New In Python 3.3.

Now that we know about the `time.monotonic()` function, let's look at how we can use it to benchmark code.

4.2 How To Benchmark

We can use the `time.monotonic()` function to benchmark code.

There are perhaps 3 case studies we may want to consider, they are:

1. Benchmarking a statement.
2. Benchmarking a function.
3. Benchmarking a program.

Let's look at how we can benchmark with the time.`monotonic()` function.

4.2.1 How To Benchmark A Statement

We can use the `time.monotonic()` function to benchmark arbitrary statements.

The procedure is as follows:

1. Record `time.monotonic()` before the statement.
2. Execute the statement.
3. Record `time.monotonic()` after the statement.
4. Subtract start time from after time to give duration.
5. Report the duration using `print()`.

For example:

```
...
# record start time
time_start = monotonic()
# execute the statement
...
# record end time
time_end = monotonic()
# calculate the duration
```

```
time_duration = time_end - time_start
# report the duration
print(f'Took {time_duration:.3f} seconds')
```

4.2.2   How To Benchmark A Function

We can use the `time.monotonic()` function to benchmark arbitrary functions.

The procedure is as follows:

1. Record `time.monotonic()` before the function.
2. Call the function.
3. Record `time.monotonic()` after the function.
4. Subtract start time from after time to give duration.
5. Report the duration using `print()`.

For example:

```
...
# record start time
time_start = monotonic()
# call the function
...
# record end time
time_end = monotonic()
# calculate the duration
time_duration = time_end - time_start
# report the duration
print(f'Took {time_duration:.3f} seconds')
```

4.2.3   How To Benchmark A Program

We can use the `time.monotonic()` function to benchmark arbitrary programs (script files).

It requires that the entry point into the program is first moved into a new function, that we will call `main()`. This is to make it easy for all code in the program to be wrapped in the benchmarking code.

The procedure is as follows:

1. Move the entry of the program into a `main()` function (if needed).
2. Record `time.monotonic()` before the `main()` function.
3. Call the `main()` function.
4. Record `time.monotonic()` after the `main()` function.
5. Subtract start time from after time to give duration.
6. Report the duration using `print()`.

For example:

```
# protect the entry point
if __name__ == '__main__':
    # record start time
    time_start = monotonic()
    # execute the program
    main()
    # record end time
    time_end = monotonic()
    # calculate the duration
    time_duration = time_end - time_start
    # report the duration
    print(f'Took {time_duration:.3f} seconds')
```

Now that we know how to benchmark using the `time.monotonic()` function, let's look at some worked examples.

4.3   Example Of Benchmarking A Statement

We can explore how to use `time.monotonic()` to benchmark a statement with a worked example.

In this example, we will define a statement that creates a list of 100 million squared integers in a list comprehension, which should take a number of seconds.

```
...
# execute the statement
data = [i*i for i in range(100000000)]
```

We will then surround this statement with benchmarking code.

Firstly, we will record the start time using the `time.monotonic()` function.

```
...
# record start time
time_start = monotonic()
```

Afterward, we will record the end time, calculate the overall execution duration, and report the result.

```
...
# record end time
time_end = monotonic()
# calculate the duration
time_duration = time_end - time_start
# report the duration
print(f'Took {time_duration:.3f} seconds')
```

Tying this together, the complete example is listed below.

```
# SuperFastPython.com
# example of benchmarking a statement with monotonic()
from time import monotonic
# record start time
time_start = monotonic()
# execute the statement
data = [i*i for i in range(100000000)]
# record end time
time_end = monotonic()
# calculate the duration
time_duration = time_end - time_start
# report the duration
print(f'Took {time_duration:.3f} seconds')
```

Running the example first records the start time, a number from an internal clock.

Next, the statement is executed, in this case creating a list of 100 million squared integers.

The end time is then recorded, as a number from an internal clock.

The difference between the two recorded times is calculated, providing the statement execution duration in seconds.

Finally, the result is reported, truncated to three decimal places (milliseconds).

In this case, we can see that the statement took about 5.070 seconds to complete.

Note, the results on your system may differ.

This highlights how we can benchmark a statement using the `time.monotonic()` function.

```
Took 5.160 seconds
```

Next, let's explore an example of benchmarking a function using the `time.monotonic()` function.

4.4 Example Of Benchmarking A Function

We can explore how to use `time.monotonic()` to benchmark a function with a worked example.

In this example, we will define a function that creates a list of 100 million squared integers in a list comprehension, which should take a number of seconds.

```
# function to benchmark
def task():
    # create a large list
    data = [i*i for i in range(100000000)]
```

We will then call this function, and surround the function call with benchmarking code.

Firstly, we will record the start time using the `time.monotonic()` function.

```
...
# record start time
time_start = monotonic()
```

Afterward, we will record the end time, calculate the overall execution duration, and report the result.

```
...
# record end time
time_end = monotonic()
# calculate the duration
time_duration = time_end - time_start
# report the duration
print(f'Took {time_duration:.3f} seconds')
```

Tying this together, the complete example is listed below.

```
# SuperFastPython.com
# example of benchmarking a function with monotonic()
from time import monotonic

# function to benchmark
def task():
    # create a large list
    data = [i*i for i in range(100000000)]

# record start time
time_start = monotonic()
# execute the function
task()
# record end time
time_end = monotonic()
# calculate the duration
time_duration = time_end - time_start
```

```
# report the duration
print(f'Took {time_duration:.3f} seconds')
```

Running the example first records the start time, a number from an internal clock.

Next, the function is called, in this case creating a list of 100 million squared integers.

The end time is then recorded, as a number from an internal clock.

The difference between the two recorded times is calculated, providing the function execution duration in seconds.

Finally, the result is reported, truncated to three decimal places (milliseconds).

In this case, we can see that the function took about 6.431 seconds to complete.

Note, the results on your system may differ.

This highlights how we can benchmark a function using the `time.monotonic()` function.

```
Took 6.112 seconds
```

Next, let's explore an example of benchmarking a program using the `time.monotonic()` function.

4.5   Example Of Benchmarking A Program

We can explore how to use `time.monotonic()` to benchmark a program with a worked example.

In this example, we will update the above example so that it has a `main()` function and protects the entry point, like a more elaborate program.

```
# main function for program
def main():
    # call a function
    task()
```

We will then add benchmarking code around the call to the `main()` function.

```
# protect the entry point
if __name__ == '__main__':
    # record start time
    time_start = monotonic()
    # execute the program
    main()
    # record end time
    time_end = monotonic()
    # calculate the duration
    time_duration = time_end - time_start
    # report the duration
    print(f'Took {time_duration:.3f} seconds')
```

Tying this together, the complete example is listed below.

```
# SuperFastPython.com
# example of benchmarking a program with monotonic()
from time import monotonic

# function to benchmark
def task():
    # create a large list
    data = [i*i for i in range(100000000)]

# main function for program
def main():
    # call a function
    task()

# protect the entry point
```

```
if __name__ == '__main__':
    # record start time
    time_start = monotonic()
    # execute the program
    main()
    # record end time
    time_end = monotonic()
    # calculate the duration
    time_duration = time_end - time_start
    # report the duration
    print(f'Took {time_duration:.3f} seconds')
```

Running the example first records the start time, a number from an internal clock.

Next, the `main()` function is called which executes the core of the program. In this case, it calls our `task()` function and creates a list of 100 million squared integers.

The end time is then recorded, as a number from an internal clock.

The difference between the two recorded times is calculated, providing the function execution duration in seconds.

Finally, the result is reported, truncated to three decimal places (milliseconds).

In this case, we can see that the function took about 6.438 seconds to complete.

Note, the results on your system may differ.

This highlights how we can benchmark a program using the `time.monotonic()` function.

```
Took 6.162 seconds
```

4.6   Example Of Checking Sleep Time

The `time.monotonic()` function does include time spent blocked or sleeping.

When the program is blocked or sleeping, the clock used by `time.monotonic()` is not paused.

We can demonstrate this with a worked example.

We can update the above example of benchmarking a statement and include a sleep for 2 seconds.

For example:

```
...
# sleep for a moment
sleep(2)
```

This will have an effect on the benchmark time, e.g. it should increase the benchmark time from about 5 seconds to about 7 seconds.

Tying this together, the complete example is listed below.

```
# SuperFastPython.com
# example of benchmarking with sleep via monotonic()
from time import monotonic
from time import sleep
# record start time
time_start = monotonic()
# execute the statement
data = [i*i for i in range(100000000)]
# sleep for a moment
sleep(2)
# record end time
time_end = monotonic()
# calculate the duration
time_duration = time_end - time_start
```

```
# report the duration
print(f'Took {time_duration:.3f} seconds')
```

Running the example, we can see that the addition of the `sleep()` after the target code does have the intended effect.

The time of the benchmark increases from about 5 seconds to about 7 seconds.

Note, the results on your system may differ.

This highlights that time spent explicitly sleeping is included in the benchmark time when using `time.monotonic()`.

```
Took 7.109 seconds
```

4.7 Example Of Checking Clock Properties

The clock used by the `time.monotonic()` function is not adjustable.

We can confirm this by reporting the details of the `"monotonic"` function in the `time` module via the `time.get_clock_info()` function.

This reports the details of the clock used by a function, like monotonic, such as whether it is adjustable, how it is implemented on the platform, whether it is monotonic, and the resolution on the platform.

The program below reports the details of the `"monotonic"` clock used by the `time.monotonic()` function.

```
# SuperFastPython.com
# details of the clock used by monotonic()
from time import get_clock_info
# get details
details = get_clock_info('monotonic')
# report details
print(details)
```

Running the program reports the details of the "monotonic" clock.

We can see that indeed it is monotonic and that the resolution on the platform is 1e-09. We can also confirm that it is not adjustable.

Note, the results on your system may differ.

This highlights how we can check the details of the clock used by a time function.

```
namespace(
    implementation='mach_absolute_time()',
    monotonic=True,
    adjustable=False,
    resolution=1e-09)
```

4.8   Further Reading

This section lists helpful additional resources on the topic.

- Monotonic function, Wikipedia.
  https://en.wikipedia.org/wiki/Monotonic_function
- `time` – Time access and conversions.
  https://docs.python.org/3/library/time.html
- What's New In Python 3.3.
  https://docs.python.org/3/whatsnew/3.3.html

4.9   Takeaways

You now know how to benchmark Python code using the `time.monotonic()` function.

Specifically, you know:

- What is the `time.monotonic()` function and its strengths and limitations when used for benchmarking.
- How to check the properties of the `time.monotonic()` function such as whether it is adjustable and monotonic.

- How to use the `time.monotonic()` function to benchmark statements, functions, and programs.

4.9.1 Next

In the next tutorial, we will explore how to benchmark with the `time.perf_counter()` function.

Chapter 5

Benchmarking With `time.perf_counter()`

You can benchmark Python code using the `time.perf_counter()` function.

In this tutorial, you will discover how to benchmark Python code using the `time.perf_counter()` function.

After completing this tutorial, you will know:

- What is the `time.perf_counter()` function and its strengths when used for benchmarking.
- How to check the properties of the `time.perf_counter()` function such as whether it is adjustable and monotonic.
- How to use the `time.perf_counter()` function to benchmark statements, functions, and programs.

Let's get started.

5.1   What Is `time.perf_counter()`

The `time.perf_counter()` function reports the value of a performance counter on the system.

It does not report the time since epoch like the `time.time()` function.

> Return the value (in fractional seconds) of a performance
> counter, i.e. a clock with the highest available resolution
> to measure a short duration. It does include time elapsed
> during sleep and is system-wide.

– `time` – Time access and conversions.

The returned value is in seconds with fractional components (e.g. milliseconds and nanoseconds), providing a high-resolution timestamp.

Calculating the difference between two timestamps from the `time.perf_counter()` allows high-resolution execution time benchmarking.

The timestamp from the `time.perf_counter()` function is consistent, meaning that two durations can be compared relative to each other in a meaningful way.

The `time.perf_counter()` function was introduced in Python version 3.3 with the intended use for short-duration benchmarking.

> `perf_counter()`: Performance counter with the highest
> available resolution to measure a short duration.

– What's New In Python 3.3.

The `time.perf_counter()` function was specifically designed to overcome the limitations of other time functions to ensure that the result is reliable, consistent, and monotonic (always increasing).

> To measure the performance of a function, `time.clock()`
> can be used but it is very different on Windows and on
> Unix. [...] The new `time.perf_counter()` function
> should be used instead to always get the most precise per-
> formance counter with a portable behaviour (ex: include
> time spend during sleep).

– PEP 418 – Add monotonic time, performance counter, and process time functions.

For accuracy, the `timeit` module (explored later in the book) makes use of the `time.perf_counter()` internally.

> The default timer, which is always `time.perf_counter()`.

– `timeit` – Measure execution time of small code snippets.

Now that we know about the `time.perf_counter()` function, let's look at how we can use it to benchmark code.

5.2 How To Benchmark

We can use the `time.perf_counter()` function to benchmark code.

There are perhaps 3 case studies we may want to consider, they are:

1. Benchmarking a statement.
2. Benchmarking a function.
3. Benchmarking a program.

Let's look at how we can benchmark with the `time.perf_counter()` function.

5.2.1 How To Benchmark A Statement

We can use the `time.perf_counter()` function to benchmark arbitrary statements.

The procedure is as follows:

1. Record `time.perf_counter()` before the statement.
2. Execute the statement.
3. Record `time.perf_counter()` after the statement.
4. Subtract start time from after time to give duration.
5. Report the duration using `print()`.

For example:

```
...
# record start time
time_start = perf_counter()
# execute the statement
```

```
. . .
# record end time
time_end = perf_counter()
# calculate the duration
time_duration = time_end - time_start
# report the duration
print(f'Took {time_duration:.3f} seconds')
```

5.2.2   How To Benchmark A Function

We can use the `time.perf_counter()` function to benchmark arbitrary functions.

The procedure is as follows:

1. Record `time.perf_counter()` before the function.
2. Call the function.
3. Record `time.perf_counter()` after the function.
4. Subtract start time from after time to give duration.
5. Report the duration using `print()`.

For example:

```
. . .
# record start time
time_start = perf_counter()
# call the function
. . .
# record end time
time_end = perf_counter()
# calculate the duration
time_duration = time_end - time_start
# report the duration
print(f'Took {time_duration:.3f} seconds')
```

5.2.3   How To Benchmark A Program

We can use the `time.perf_counter()` function to benchmark arbitrary programs (script files).

It requires that the entry point into the program is first moved into a new function, that we will call `main()`. This is to make it easy for all code in the program to be wrapped in the benchmarking code.

The procedure is as follows:

1. Move the entry of the program into a `main()` function (if needed).
2. Record `time.perf_counter()` before the `main()` function.
3. Call the `main()` function.
4. Record `time.perf_counter()` after the `main()` function.
5. Subtract start time from after time to give duration.
6. Report the duration using `print()`.

For example:

```
# protect the entry point
if __name__ == '__main__':
    # record start time
    time_start = perf_counter()
    # execute the program
    main()
    # record end time
    time_end = perf_counter()
    # calculate the duration
    time_duration = time_end - time_start
    # report the duration
    print(f'Took {time_duration:.3f} seconds')
```

Now that we know how to benchmark using the `time.perf_counter()` function, let's look at some worked examples.

5.3 Example Of Benchmarking A Statement

We can explore how to use `time.perf_counter()` to benchmark a statement with a worked example.

In this example, we will define a statement that creates a list of 100 million squared integers in a list comprehension, which should take a number of seconds.

```
...
# execute the statement
data = [i*i for i in range(100000000)]
```

We will then surround this statement with benchmarking code.

Firstly, we will record the start time using the `time.perf_counter()` function.

```
...
# record start time
time_start = perf_counter()
```

Afterward, we will record the end time, calculate the overall execution duration, and report the result.

```
...
# record end time
time_end = perf_counter()
# calculate the duration
time_duration = time_end - time_start
# report the duration
print(f'Took {time_duration:.3f} seconds')
```

Tying this together, the complete example is listed below.

```
# SuperFastPython.com
# example of benchmarking statement with perf_counter()
from time import perf_counter
# record start time
time_start = perf_counter()
# execute the statement
data = [i*i for i in range(100000000)]
# record end time
time_end = perf_counter()
# calculate the duration
time_duration = time_end - time_start
```

```
# report the duration
print(f'Took {time_duration:.3f} seconds')
```

Running the example first records the start time, a number from an internal high-performance counter.

Next, the statement is executed, in this case creating a list of 100 million squared integers.

The end time is then recorded, as a number from an internal high-performance counter.

The difference between the two recorded times is calculated, providing the statement execution duration in seconds.

Finally, the result is reported, truncated to three decimal places (milliseconds).

In this case, we can see that the statement took about 5.070 seconds to complete.

Note, the results on your system may differ.

This highlights how we can benchmark a statement using the `time.perf_counter()` function.

```
Took 5.070 seconds
```

Next, let's explore an example of benchmarking a function using the `time.perf_counter()` function.

5.4 Example Of Benchmarking A Function

We can explore how to use `time.perf_counter()` to benchmark a function with a worked example.

In this example, we will define a function that creates a list of 100 million squared integers in a list comprehension, which should take a number of seconds.

```
# function to benchmark
def task():
    # create a large list
    data = [i*i for i in range(100000000)]
```

We will then call this function, and surround the function call with benchmarking code.

Firstly, we will record the start time using the `time.perf_counter()` function.

```
...
# record start time
time_start = perf_counter()
```

Afterward, we will record the end time, calculate the overall execution duration, and report the result.

```
...
# record end time
time_end = perf_counter()
# calculate the duration
time_duration = time_end - time_start
# report the duration
print(f'Took {time_duration:.3f} seconds')
```

Tying this together, the complete example is listed below.

```
# SuperFastPython.com
# example of benchmarking a function with perf_counter()
from time import perf_counter

# function to benchmark
def task():
    # create a large list
    data = [i*i for i in range(100000000)]

# record start time
time_start = perf_counter()
# execute the function
```

```
task()
# record end time
time_end = perf_counter()
# calculate the duration
time_duration = time_end - time_start
# report the duration
print(f'Took {time_duration:.3f} seconds')
```

Running the example first records the start time, a number from an internal high-performance counter.

Next, the function is called, in this case creating a list of 100 million squared integers.

The end time is then recorded, as a number from an internal high-performance counter.

The difference between the two recorded times is calculated, providing the function execution duration in seconds.

Finally, the result is reported, truncated to three decimal places (milliseconds).

In this case, we can see that the function took about 6.431 seconds to complete.

Note, the results on your system may differ.

This highlights how we can benchmark a function using the `time.perf_counter()` function.

```
Took 6.431 seconds
```

Next, let's explore an example of benchmarking a program using the `time.perf_counter()` function.

5.5　Example Of Benchmarking A Program

We can explore how to use `time.perf_counter()` to benchmark a program with a worked example.

In this example, we will update the above example so that it has a `main()` function and protects the entry point, like a more elaborate program.

```
# main function for program
def main():
    # call a function
    task()
```

We will then add benchmarking code around the call to the `main()` function.

```
# protect the entry point
if __name__ == '__main__':
    # record start time
    time_start = perf_counter()
    # execute the program
    main()
    # record end time
    time_end = perf_counter()
    # calculate the duration
    time_duration = time_end - time_start
    # report the duration
    print(f'Took {time_duration:.3f} seconds')
```

Tying this together, the complete example is listed below.

```
# SuperFastPython.com
# example of benchmarking a program with perf_counter()
from time import perf_counter

# function to benchmark
def task():
```

```
    # create a large list
    data = [i*i for i in range(100000000)]

# main function for program
def main():
    # call a function
    task()

# protect the entry point
if __name__ == '__main__':
    # record start time
    time_start = perf_counter()
    # execute the program
    main()
    # record end time
    time_end = perf_counter()
    # calculate the duration
    time_duration = time_end - time_start
    # report the duration
    print(f'Took {time_duration:.3f} seconds')
```

Running the example first records the start time, a number from an internal high-performance counter.

Next, the `main()` function is called which executes the core of the program. In this case, it calls our `task()` function and creates a list of 100 million squared integers.

The end time is then recorded, as a number from an internal high-performance counter.

The difference between the two recorded times is calculated, providing the function execution duration in seconds.

Finally, the result is reported, truncated to three decimal places (milliseconds).

In this case, we can see that the function took about 6.438 seconds to complete.

Note, the results on your system may differ.

This highlights how we can benchmark a program using the `time.perf_counter()` function.

```
Took 6.438 seconds
```

5.6   Example Of Checking Sleep Time

The `time.perf_counter()` function does include time spent blocked or sleeping.

When the program is blocked or sleeping, the clock used by `time.perf_counter()` is not paused.

We can demonstrate this with a worked example.

We can update the above example of benchmarking a statement and include a sleep for 2 seconds.

For example:

```
...
# sleep for a moment
sleep(2)
```

This will have an effect on the benchmark time, e.g. it should increase the benchmark time from about 5 seconds to about 7 seconds.

Tying this together, the complete example is listed below.

```
# SuperFastPython.com
# example of benchmarking with sleep via perf_counter()
from time import perf_counter
from time import sleep
# record start time
time_start = perf_counter()
# execute the statement
data = [i*i for i in range(100000000)]
# sleep for a moment
sleep(2)
```

```
# record end time
time_end = perf_counter()
# calculate the duration
time_duration = time_end - time_start
# report the duration
print(f'Took {time_duration:.3f} seconds')
```

Running the example, we can see that the addition of the `sleep()` after the target code does have the intended effect.

The time of the benchmark increases from about 5 seconds to about 7 seconds.

Note, the results on your system may differ.

This highlights that time spent explicitly sleeping is included in the benchmark time when using `time.perf_counter()`.

```
Took 7.092 seconds
```

5.7   Example Of Checking Clock Properties

The clock used by the `time.perf_counter()` function is not adjustable.

This means that the system will not change the clock while our program is running.

Because the clock cannot be adjusted, it means that it is monotonic. This means that all future values of the clock will be after past values of the clock.

We can confirm this by reporting the details of the `"perf_counter"` function in the `time` module via the `time.get_clock_info()` function.

This reports the details of the clock used by a time function, such as whether it is adjustable, how it is implemented on the platform,

73

whether it is monotonic, and the resolution on the platform.

The program below reports the details of the **"perf_counter"** clock used by the **time.perf_counter()** function.

```
# SuperFastPython.com
# details of the clock used by perf_counter()
from time import get_clock_info
# get details
details = get_clock_info('perf_counter')
# report details
print(details)
```

Running the program reports the details of the **"perf_counter"** clock.

We can see that indeed it is monotonic and that the resolution on the platform is 1e-09. We can also confirm that it is not adjustable.

Note, the results on your system may differ.

This highlights how we can check the details of the clock used by a time function.

```
namespace(
    implementation='mach_absolute_time()',
    monotonic=True,
    adjustable=False,
    resolution=1e-09)
```

5.8   Further Reading

This section lists helpful additional resources on the topic.

- **time** – Time access and conversions.
  https://docs.python.org/3/library/time.html
- What's New In Python 3.3.
  https://docs.python.org/3/whatsnew/3.3.html
- PEP 418 – Add monotonic time, performance counter, and process time functions.

https://peps.python.org/pep-0418/
- `timeit` – Measure execution time of small code snippets. https://docs.python.org/3/library/timeit.html

5.9 Takeaways

You now know how to benchmark Python code using the `time.perf_counter()` function.

Specifically, you know:

- What is the `time.perf_counter()` function and its strengths when used for benchmarking.
- How to check the properties of the `time.perf_counter()` function such as whether it is adjustable and monotonic.
- How to use the `time.perf_counter()` function to benchmark statements, functions, and programs.

5.9.1 Next

In the next tutorial, we will explore how to benchmark with the `time.thread_time()` function.

Chapter 6

Benchmarking With `time.thread_time()`

You can benchmark Python code using the `time.thread_time()` function.

In this tutorial, you will discover how to benchmark Python code using the `time.thread_time()` function.

After completing this tutorial, you will know:

- What is the `time.thread_time()` function and its strengths and limitations when used for benchmarking.
- How to check the properties of the `time.thread_time()` function such as whether it is adjustable and monotonic.
- How to use the `time.thread_time()` function to benchmark statements, functions, and programs.

Let's get started.

6.1 What Is `time.thread_time()`

We can benchmark code using the `time.thread_time()` function.

This is a function that is provided in the **time** module and is part of the Python standard library.

The `time.thread_time()` function returns the time that the current thread has been executing in seconds.

The time begins or is zero when the current thread is first created.

> Return the value (in fractional seconds) of the sum of the system and user CPU time of the current thread.

– `time` – Time access and conversions.

It is an equivalent value to the `time.process_time()`, except calculated for the scope of the current thread, not the current process.

This value is calculated as the sum of the system time and the user time.

- thread time = user time + system time

The reported time does not include sleep time.

This means if the thread is blocked by a call to `time.sleep()` or perhaps is suspended by the operating system, then this time is not included in the reported time. This is called a "thread-wide" or "thread-specific" time.

> It does not include time elapsed during sleep.

– `time` – Time access and conversions.

The `time.thread_time()` function was added in Python version 3.7.

> The new `time.thread_time()` and `time.thread_time_ns()` functions can be used to get per-thread CPU time measurements.

– What's New In Python 3.7.

Now that we know about the `time.thread_time()` function, let's look at how we can use it to benchmark our Python programs.

6.2   How To Benchmark

We can use the `time.thread_time()` function to benchmark code.

There are perhaps 3 case studies we may want to consider, they are:

1. Benchmarking a statement.
2. Benchmarking a function.
3. Benchmarking a program.

Let's look at how we can benchmark `time.thread_time()` function.

6.2.1   How To Benchmark A Statement

We can use the `time.thread_time()` function to benchmark arbitrary statements.

The procedure is as follows:

1. Record `time.thread_time()` before the statement.
2. Execute the statement.
3. Record `time.thread_time()` after the statement.
4. Subtract start time from after time to give duration.
5. Report the duration using `print()`.

For example:

```
...
# record start time
time_start = thread_time()
# execute the statement
...
# record end time
time_end = thread_time()
# calculate the duration
time_duration = time_end - time_start
# report the duration
print(f'Took {time_duration:.3f} seconds')
```

6.2.2   How To Benchmark A Function

We can use the `time.thread_time()` function to benchmark arbitrary functions.

The procedure is as follows:

1. Record `time.thread_time()` before the function.
2. Call the function.
3. Record `time.thread_time()` after the function.
4. Subtract start time from after time to give duration.
5. Report the duration using `print()`.

For example:

```
...
# record start time
time_start = thread_time()
# call the function
...
# record end time
time_end = thread_time()
# calculate the duration
time_duration = time_end - time_start
# report the duration
print(f'Took {time_duration:.3f} seconds')
```

6.2.3   How To Benchmark A Program

We can use the `time.thread_time()` function to benchmark arbitrary programs (script files).

It requires that the entry point into the program is first moved into a new function, that we will call `main()`. This is to make it easy for all code in the program to be wrapped in the benchmarking code.

The procedure is as follows:

1. Move the entry of the program into a `main()` function (if needed).
2. Record `time.thread_time()` before the `main()` function.

3. Call the `main()` function.
4. Record `time.thread_time()` after the `main()` function.
5. Subtract start time from after time to give duration.
6. Report the duration using `print()`.

For example:

```
# protect the entry point
if __name__ == '__main__':
    # record start time
    time_start = thread_time()
    # execute the program
    main()
    # record end time
    time_end = thread_time()
    # calculate the duration
    time_duration = time_end - time_start
    # report the duration
    print(f'Took {time_duration:.3f} seconds')
```

Now that we know how to benchmark using the `time.thread_time()` function, let's look at some worked examples.

6.3   Example Of Benchmarking A Statement

We can explore how to use `time.thread_time()` to benchmark a statement with a worked example.

In this example, we will define a statement that creates a list of 100 million squared integers in a list comprehension, which should take a number of seconds.

```
...
# execute the statement
data = [i*i for i in range(100000000)]
```

We will then surround this statement with benchmarking code.

Firstly, we will record the start time using the `time.thread_time()` function.

```
...
# record start time
time_start = thread_time()
```

Afterward, we will record the end time, calculate the overall execution duration, and report the result.

```
...
# record end time
time_end = thread_time()
# calculate the duration
time_duration = time_end - time_start
# report the duration
print(f'Took {time_duration:.3f} seconds')
```

Tying this together, the complete example is listed below.

```
# SuperFastPython.com
# example of benchmarking a statement with thread_time()
from time import thread_time
# record start time
time_start = thread_time()
# execute the statement
data = [i*i for i in range(100000000)]
# record end time
time_end = thread_time()
# calculate the duration
time_duration = time_end - time_start
# report the duration
print(f'Took {time_duration:.3f} seconds')
```

Running the example first records the start time, a number from an internal clock for the thread.

Next, the statement is executed, in this case creating a list of 100 million squared integers.

The end time is then recorded, as a number from an internal clock for the thread.

The difference between the two recorded times is calculated, providing the statement execution duration in seconds.

Finally, the result is reported, truncated to three decimal places (milliseconds).

In this case, we can see that the statement took about 5.070 seconds to complete.

Note, the results on your system may differ.

This highlights how we can benchmark a statement using the `time.thread_time()` function.

```
Took 5.118 seconds
```

Next, let's explore an example of benchmarking a function using the `time.thread_time()` function.

6.4 Example Of Benchmarking A Function

We can explore how to use `time.thread_time()` to benchmark a function with a worked example.

In this example, we will define a function that creates a list of 100 million squared integers in a list comprehension, which should take a number of seconds.

```
# function to benchmark
def task():
    # create a large list
    data = [i*i for i in range(100000000)]
```

We will then call this function, and surround the function call with benchmarking code.

Firstly, we will record the start time using the `time.thread_time()` function.

```
...
# record start time
time_start = thread_time()
```

Afterward, we will record the end time, calculate the overall execution duration, and report the result.

```
...
# record end time
time_end = thread_time()
# calculate the duration
time_duration = time_end - time_start
# report the duration
print(f'Took {time_duration:.3f} seconds')
```

Tying this together, the complete example is listed below.

```
# SuperFastPython.com
# example of benchmarking a function with thread_time()
from time import thread_time

# function to benchmark
def task():
    # create a large list
    data = [i*i for i in range(100000000)]

# record start time
time_start = thread_time()
# execute the function
task()
# record end time
time_end = thread_time()
# calculate the duration
time_duration = time_end - time_start
# report the duration
print(f'Took {time_duration:.3f} seconds')
```

Running the example first records the start time, a number from an internal clock for the thread.

Next, the function is called, in this case creating a list of 100 million squared integers.

The end time is then recorded, as a number from an internal clock for the thread.

The difference between the two recorded times is calculated, providing the function execution duration in seconds.

Finally, the result is reported, truncated to three decimal places (milliseconds).

In this case, we can see that the function took about 6.431 seconds to complete.

Note, the results on your system may differ.

This highlights how we can benchmark a function using the `time.thread_time()` function.

```
Took 6.194 seconds
```

Next, let's explore an example of benchmarking a program using the `time.thread_time()` function.

6.5   Example Of Benchmarking A Program

We can explore how to use `time.thread_time()` to benchmark a program with a worked example.

In this example, we will update the above example so that it has a `main()` function and protects the entry point, like a more elaborate program.

```
# main function for program
def main():
    # call a function
    task()
```

We will then add benchmarking code around the call to the `main()` function.

```python
# protect the entry point
if __name__ == '__main__':
    # record start time
    time_start = thread_time()
    # execute the program
    main()
    # record end time
    time_end = thread_time()
    # calculate the duration
    time_duration = time_end - time_start
    # report the duration
    print(f'Took {time_duration:.3f} seconds')
```

Tying this together, the complete example is listed below.

```python
# SuperFastPython.com
# example of benchmarking a program with thread_time()
from time import thread_time

# function to benchmark
def task():
    # create a large list
    data = [i*i for i in range(100000000)]

# main function for program
def main():
    # call a function
    task()

# protect the entry point
if __name__ == '__main__':
    # record start time
    time_start = thread_time()
    # execute the program
    main()
```

```
# record end time
time_end = thread_time()
# calculate the duration
time_duration = time_end - time_start
# report the duration
print(f'Took {time_duration:.3f} seconds')
```

Running the example first records the start time, a number from an internal clock for the thread.

Next, the **main()** function is called which executes the core of the program. In this case, it calls our **task()** function and creates a list of 100 million squared integers.

The end time is then recorded, as a number from an internal clock for the thread.

The difference between the two recorded times is calculated, providing the function execution duration in seconds.

Finally, the result is reported, truncated to three decimal places (milliseconds).

In this case, we can see that the function took about 6.438 seconds to complete.

Note, the results on your system may differ.

This highlights how we can benchmark a program using the **time.thread_time()** function.

```
Took 6.199 seconds
```

6.6   Example Of Checking Sleep Time

The **time.thread_time()** function does not include time spent blocked or sleeping.

When the thread is blocked or sleeping, the clock used by **time.thread_time()** is paused. When the program is resumed, the clock used by **time.thread_time()** is then also resumed.

This means benchmarking performed using the `time.thread_time()` function will exclude time spent sleeping or blocked.

We can demonstrate this with a worked example.

We can update the above example of benchmarking a statement and include a sleep for 2 seconds.

For example:

```
...
# sleep for a moment
sleep(2)
```

This will have an effect on the benchmark time, e.g. it will not increase the benchmark time from about 5 seconds to about 7 seconds as we might naively expect

Tying this together, the complete example is listed below.

```
# SuperFastPython.com
# example of benchmarking with sleep via thread_time()
from time import thread_time
from time import sleep
# record start time
time_start = thread_time()
# execute the statement
data = [i*i for i in range(100000000)]
# sleep for a moment
sleep(2)
# record end time
time_end = thread_time()
# calculate the duration
time_duration = time_end - time_start
# report the duration
print(f'Took {time_duration:.3f} seconds')
```

Running the example, we can see that the addition of the `sleep()` after the target code does have the intended effect.

The time of the overall benchmark duration does not increase by the added sleep time, e.g. from 5 to 7 seconds.

Note, the results on your system may differ.

This highlights that time spent explicitly sleeping is excluded in the benchmark time when using `time.thread_time()`.

```
Took 5.111 seconds
```

6.7 Example Of Checking Clock Properties

The clock used by the `time.thread_time()` function is not adjustable.

We can confirm this by reporting the details of the `"thread_time"` function in the `time` module via the `time.get_clock_info()` function.

This reports the details of the clock used by a function, like thread_time, such as whether it is adjustable, how it is implemented on the platform, whether it is thread_time, and the resolution on the platform.

The program below reports the details of the `"thread_time"` clock used by the `time.thread_time()` function.

```
# SuperFastPython.com
# details of the clock used by thread_time()
from time import get_clock_info
# get details
details = get_clock_info('thread_time')
# report details
print(details)
```

Running the program reports the details of the `"thread_time"` clock.

We can see that indeed it is monotonic and that the resolution on the platform is 1e-09. We can also confirm that it is not adjustable.

Note, the results on your system may differ.

This highlights how we can check the details of the clock used by a time function.

```
namespace(implementation='clock_gettime(
        CLOCK_THREAD_CPUTIME_ID)',
    monotonic=True,
    adjustable=False,
    resolution=1e-09)
```

6.8   Further Reading

This section lists helpful additional resources on the topic.

- `time` – Time access and conversions.
  https://docs.python.org/3/library/time.html
- What's New In Python 3.7.
  https://docs.python.org/3/whatsnew/3.7.html

6.9   Takeaways

You now know how to benchmark Python code using the `time.thread_time()` function.

Specifically, you know:

- What is the `time.thread_time()` function and its strengths and limitations when used for benchmarking.
- How to check the properties of the `time.thread_time()` function such as whether it is adjustable and monotonic.
- How to use the `time.thread_time()` function to benchmark statements, functions, and programs.

6.9.1   Next

In the next tutorial, we will explore how to benchmark with the `time.process_time()` function.

Chapter 7

Benchmarking With `time.process_time()`

You can benchmark Python code using the `time.process_time()` function.

In this tutorial, you will discover how to benchmark Python code using the `time.process_time()` function.

After completing this tutorial, you will know:

- What is the `time.process_time()` function and its strengths and limitations when used for benchmarking.
- How to check the properties of the `time.process_time()` function such as whether it is adjustable and monotonic.
- How to use the `time.process_time()` function to benchmark statements, functions, and programs.

Let's get started.

7.1 What Is `time.process_time()`

We can benchmark code using the `time.process_time()` function.

This is a function that is provided in the **time** module and is part of

91

the Python standard library.

The `time.process_time()` function returns the time that the current process has been executing in seconds.

The time begins or is zero when the current process is first created.

> Return the value (in fractional seconds) of the sum of the system and user CPU time of the current process.

– `time` – Time access and conversions.

This value is calculated as the sum of the system time and the user time.

- process time = user time + system time

Recall system time is time that the CPU is spent executing system calls for the kernel (e.g. the operating system), whereas user time is time spent by the CPU executing calls in the program (e.g. our code).

> When a program loops through an array, it is accumulating user CPU time. Conversely, when a program executes a system call such as exec or fork, it is accumulating system CPU time.

– time (Unix), Wikipedia.

The reported time does not include sleep time.

This means if the process is blocked by a call to `time.sleep()` or perhaps is suspended by the operating system, then this time is not included in the reported time. This is called a "process-wide" time.

> It does not include time elapsed during sleep.

– `time` – Time access and conversions.

As such, it only reports the time that the current process was executed since it was created by the operating system.

The `time.process_time()` function was proposed in *PEP 418 – Add monotonic time, performance counter, and process time functions.*

> The new `time.process_time()` function acts as a portable counter that always measures CPU time (excluding time elapsed during sleep) and has the best available resolution.

– PEP 418 – Add monotonic time, performance counter, and process time functions.

It was then added to Python in version 3.3.

> `process_time()`: Sum of the system and user CPU time of the current process.

– What's New In Python 3.3.

Now that we know about the `time.process_time()` function, let's look at how we can use it to benchmark our programs.

7.2   How To Benchmark

We can use the `time.process_time()` function to benchmark code.

There are perhaps 3 case studies we may want to consider, they are:

1. Benchmarking a statement.
2. Benchmarking a function.
3. Benchmarking a program.

Let's look at how we can benchmark `time.process_time()` function.

7.2.1   How To Benchmark A Statement

We can use the `time.process_time()` function to benchmark arbitrary statements.

The procedure is as follows:

1. Record `time.process_time()` before the statement.
2. Execute the statement.
3. Record `time.process_time()` after the statement.
4. Subtract start time from after time to give duration.

5. Report the duration using `print()`.

For example:

```
...
# record start time
time_start = process_time()
# execute the statement
...
# record end time
time_end = process_time()
# calculate the duration
time_duration = time_end - time_start
# report the duration
print(f'Took {time_duration:.3f} seconds')
```

7.2.2   How To Benchmark A Function

We can use the `time.process_time()` function to benchmark arbitrary functions.

The procedure is as follows:

1. Record `time.process_time()` before the function.
2. Call the function.
3. Record `time.process_time()` after the function.
4. Subtract start time from after time to give duration.
5. Report the duration using `print()`.

For example:

```
...
# record start time
time_start = process_time()
# call the function
...
# record end time
time_end = process_time()
# calculate the duration
time_duration = time_end - time_start
```

```
# report the duration
print(f'Took {time_duration:.3f} seconds')
```

7.2.3 How To Benchmark A Program

We can use the `time.process_time()` function to benchmark arbitrary programs (script files).

It requires that the entry point into the program is first moved into a new function, that we will call `main()`. This is to make it easy for all code in the program to be wrapped in the benchmarking code.

The procedure is as follows:

1. Move the entry of the program into a `main()` function (if needed).
2. Record `time.process_time()` before the `main()` function.
3. Call the `main()` function.
4. Record `time.process_time()` after the `main()` function.
5. Subtract start time from after time to give duration.
6. Report the duration using `print()`.

For example:

```
# protect the entry point
if __name__ == '__main__':
    # record start time
    time_start = process_time()
    # execute the program
    main()
    # record end time
    time_end = process_time()
    # calculate the duration
    time_duration = time_end - time_start
    # report the duration
    print(f'Took {time_duration:.3f} seconds')
```

Now that we know how to benchmark using the `time.process_time()` function, let's look at some worked examples.

7.3 Example Of Benchmarking A Statement

We can explore how to use `time.process_time()` to benchmark a statement with a worked example.

In this example, we will define a statement that creates a list of 100 million squared integers in a list comprehension, which should take a number of seconds.

```
...
# execute the statement
data = [i*i for i in range(100000000)]
```

We will then surround this statement with benchmarking code.

Firstly, we will record the start time using the `time.process_time()` function.

```
...
# record start time
time_start = process_time()
```

Afterward, we will record the end time, calculate the overall execution duration, and report the result.

```
...
# record end time
time_end = process_time()
# calculate the duration
time_duration = time_end - time_start
# report the duration
print(f'Took {time_duration:.3f} seconds')
```

Tying this together, the complete example is listed below.

```
# SuperFastPython.com
# example of benchmarking statement with process_time()
from time import process_time
# record start time
time_start = process_time()
# execute the statement
```

```
data = [i*i for i in range(100000000)]
# record end time
time_end = process_time()
# calculate the duration
time_duration = time_end - time_start
# report the duration
print(f'Took {time_duration:.3f} seconds')
```

Running the example first records the start time, a number from an internal clock for the process.

Next, the statement is executed, in this case creating a list of 100 million squared integers.

The end time is then recorded, as a number from an internal clock for the process.

The difference between the two recorded times is calculated, providing the statement execution duration in seconds.

Finally, the result is reported, truncated to three decimal places (milliseconds).

In this case, we can see that the statement took about 5.070 seconds to complete.

Note, the results on your system may differ.

This highlights how we can benchmark a statement using the `time.process_time()` function.

```
Took 5.073 seconds
```

Next, let's explore an example of benchmarking a function using the `time.process_time()` function.

7.4 Example Of Benchmarking A Function

We can explore how to use `time.process_time()` to benchmark a function with a worked example.

In this example, we will define a function that creates a list of 100 million squared integers in a list comprehension, which should take a number of seconds.

```
# function to benchmark
def task():
    # create a large list
    data = [i*i for i in range(100000000)]
```

We will then call this function, and surround the function call with benchmarking code.

Firstly, we will record the start time using the `time.process_time()` function.

```
...
# record start time
time_start = process_time()
```

Afterward, we will record the end time, calculate the overall execution duration, and report the result.

```
...
# record end time
time_end = process_time()
# calculate the duration
time_duration = time_end - time_start
# report the duration
print(f'Took {time_duration:.3f} seconds')
```

Tying this together, the complete example is listed below.

```
# SuperFastPython.com
# example of benchmarking a function with process_time()
from time import process_time
```

```
# function to benchmark
def task():
    # create a large list
    data = [i*i for i in range(100000000)]

# record start time
time_start = process_time()
# execute the function
task()
# record end time
time_end = process_time()
# calculate the duration
time_duration = time_end - time_start
# report the duration
print(f'Took {time_duration:.3f} seconds')
```

Running the example first records the start time, a number from an internal clock for the process.

Next, the function is called, in this case creating a list of 100 million squared integers.

The end time is then recorded, as a number from an internal clock for the process.

The difference between the two recorded times is calculated, providing the function execution duration in seconds.

Finally, the result is reported, truncated to three decimal places (milliseconds).

In this case, we can see that the function took about 6.431 seconds to complete.

Note, the results on your system may differ.

This highlights how we can benchmark a function using the `time.process_time()` function.

```
Took 6.249 seconds
```

Next, let's explore an example of benchmarking a program using the `time.process_time()` function.

7.5 Example Of Benchmarking A Program

We can explore how to use `time.process_time()` to benchmark a program with a worked example.

In this example, we will update the above example so that it has a `main()` function and protects the entry point, like a more elaborate program.

```
# main function for program
def main():
    # call a function
    task()
```

We will then add benchmarking code around the call to the `main()` function.

```
# protect the entry point
if __name__ == '__main__':
    # record start time
    time_start = process_time()
    # execute the program
    main()
    # record end time
    time_end = process_time()
    # calculate the duration
    time_duration = time_end - time_start
    # report the duration
    print(f'Took {time_duration:.3f} seconds')
```

Tying this together, the complete example is listed below.

```
# SuperFastPython.com
# example of benchmarking a program with process_time()
from time import process_time

# function to benchmark
def task():
    # create a large list
    data = [i*i for i in range(100000000)]

# main function for program
def main():
    # call a function
    task()

# protect the entry point
if __name__ == '__main__':
    # record start time
    time_start = process_time()
    # execute the program
    main()
    # record end time
    time_end = process_time()
    # calculate the duration
    time_duration = time_end - time_start
    # report the duration
    print(f'Took {time_duration:.3f} seconds')
```

Running the example first records the start time, a number from an internal clock for the process.

Next, the `main()` function is called which executes the core of the program. In this case, it calls our `task()` function and creates a list of 100 million squared integers.

The end time is then recorded, as a number from an internal clock for the process.

The difference between the two recorded times is calculated, providing the function execution duration in seconds.

Finally, the result is reported, truncated to three decimal places (milliseconds).

In this case, we can see that the function took about 6.438 seconds to complete.

Note, the results on your system may differ.

This highlights how we can benchmark a program using the time.process_time() function.

```
Took 6.149 seconds
```

7.6 Example Of Checking Sleep Time

The time.process_time() function does not include time spent blocked or sleeping.

When the program is blocked or sleeping, the clock used by time.process_time() is paused. When the program is resumed, the clock used by time.process_time() is then also resumed.

This means benchmarking performed using the time.process_time() function will exclude time spent sleeping or blocked.

We can demonstrate this with a worked example.

We can update the example of benchmarking a statement and include a sleep for 2 seconds.

For example:

```
...
# sleep for a moment
sleep(2)
```

This will have an effect on the benchmark time, e.g. it will not increase the benchmark time from about 5 seconds to about 7 seconds as we might naively expect

Tying this together, the complete example is listed below.

```
# SuperFastPython.com
# example of benchmarking with sleep via process_time()
from time import process_time
from time import sleep
# record start time
time_start = process_time()
# execute the statement
data = [i*i for i in range(100000000)]
# sleep for a moment
sleep(2)
# record end time
time_end = process_time()
# calculate the duration
time_duration = time_end - time_start
# report the duration
print(f'Took {time_duration:.3f} seconds')
```

Running the example, we can see that the addition of the `sleep()` after the target code does have the intended effect.

The time of the overall benchmark duration does not increase by the added sleep time, e.g. from 5 to 7 seconds.

Note, the results on your system may differ.

This highlights that time spent explicitly sleeping is excluded in the benchmark time when using `time.process_time()`.

```
Took 5.151 seconds
```

7.7 Example Of Checking Clock Properties

The clock used by the `time.process_time()` function is not adjustable.

We can confirm this by reporting the details of the `"process_time"` function in the `time` module via the `time.get_clock_info()` function.

This reports the details of the clock used by a function, like process_time, such as whether it is adjustable, how it is implemented on the platform, whether it is process_time, and the resolution on the platform.

The program below reports the details of the "process_time" clock used by the time.process_time() function.

```
# SuperFastPython.com
# details of the clock used by process_time()
from time import get_clock_info
# get details
details = get_clock_info('process_time')
# report details
print(details)
```

Running the program reports the details of the "process_time" clock.

We can see that indeed it is monotonic and that the resolution on the platform is 1.0000000000000002e-06.

We can also confirm that it is not adjustable. Note, the results on your system may differ.

This highlights how we can check the details of the clock used by a time function.

```
namespace(implementation='clock_gettime(
        CLOCK_PROCESS_CPUTIME_ID)',
    monotonic=True,
    adjustable=False,
    resolution=1.0000000000000002e-06)
```

7.8   Further Reading

This section lists helpful additional resources on the topic.

- time (Unix), Wikipedia.
  https://en.wikipedia.org/wiki/Time_(Unix)
- time – Time access and conversions.
  https://docs.python.org/3/library/time.html
- PEP 418 – Add monotonic time, performance counter, and process time functions.
  https://peps.python.org/pep-0418
- What's New In Python 3.3.
  https://docs.python.org/3/whatsnew/3.3.html

7.9 Takeaways

You now know how to benchmark Python code using the `time.process_time()` function.

Specifically, you know:

- What is the `time.process_time()` function and its strengths and limitations when used for benchmarking.
- How to check the properties of the `time.process_time()` function such as whether it is adjustable and monotonic.
- How to use the `time.process_time()` function to benchmark statements, functions, and programs.

7.9.1 Next

In the next tutorial, we will explore how to compare the time functions in the `time` module.

Chapter 8

Comparing `time` Module Functions

You can benchmark the execution of Python code using functions in the `time` module in the standard library.

In this tutorial, you will discover how to time the execution of Python code using a suite of different time functions.

After completing this tutorial, you will know:

- How the details of each of the 5 time functions compare, such as adjustable, monotonic, and resolution.
- How to compare the `time.time()` and `time.perf_counter()` functions and when to use each.
- How to choose time functions for benchmarking and other tasks such as waiting and timeouts.

Let's get started.

8.1 Example Of Comparing Time Function Clocks

As we have seen in previous chapters, there are 5 ways to measure execution time in Python using the `time` module, they are:

1. Use `time.time()`
2. Use `time.perf_counter()`
3. Use `time.monotonic()`
4. Use `time.process_time()`
5. Use `time.thread_time()`

The differences between these time functions can be confusing.

Helpfully, the `time.get_clock_info(name)` function can be used to report the technical details of the clock used by each `time` module function.

The program below reports these details.

```python
# SuperFastPython.com
# report the details of each time function
from time import get_clock_info
# time.time()
print(get_clock_info('time'))
# time.perf_counter()
print(get_clock_info('perf_counter'))
# time.monotonic()
print(get_clock_info('monotonic'))
# time.process_time()
print(get_clock_info('process_time'))
# time.thread_time()
print(get_clock_info('thread_time'))
```

Running the program reports the following details:

Note, the results on your system may differ.

```python
namespace(
    implementation='clock_gettime(CLOCK_REALTIME)',
```

```
    monotonic=False,
    adjustable=True,
    resolution=1.0000000000000002e-06)
namespace(
    implementation='mach_absolute_time()',
    monotonic=True,
    adjustable=False,
    resolution=1e-09)
namespace(
    implementation='mach_absolute_time()',
    monotonic=True,
    adjustable=False,
    resolution=1e-09)
namespace(implementation='clock_gettime(
    CLOCK_PROCESS_CPUTIME_ID)',
    monotonic=True,
    adjustable=False,
    resolution=1.0000000000000002e-06)
namespace(implementation='clock_gettime(
    CLOCK_THREAD_CPUTIME_ID)',
    monotonic=True,
    adjustable=False,
    resolution=1e-09)
```

We can collect these details into a readable table, below.

Note, the resolution values have been simplified for brevity.

This table may help tease apart their important details.

Function	Scope	Monotonic	Adjusted	Resolution
time()	System	No	Yes	1e-06
perf_counter()	System	Yes	No	1e-09
monotonic()	System	Yes	No	1e-09
process_time()	Process	Yes	No	1e-06
thread_time()	Thread	Yes	No	1e-09

Scope refers to the point of reference for the time calculation. Most time functions are system-wide, meaning that different Python programs can access the same underlying clock and retrieve comparable times if needed.

Monotonic refers to whether subsequent calls always result in a larger return value or not. We can see that `time.time()` is not monotonic, because it could be adjusted.

Adjustable refers to the fact that the clock on which the time is based may be modified, e.g. updated manually or automatically. This can impact the relative difference between two times if the underlying clock jumps around by a seconds, minutes, or hours.

The resolution provides an idea of the number of clock ticks that may be measured within one second, also called the sampling rate. A smaller number means a higher resolution (better), perhaps at some computational cost. We can see that `perf_counter()` and `monotonic()` are high-resolution, whereas `time.process_time()` and `time.time()` are lower-resolution. These values may differ across different operating systems and hardware systems.

Generally, `time.time()` should be avoided for benchmarking because it could be adjusted by the system while being used. Nevertheless, it is widely used for benchmarking.

The `time.perf_counter()` and `time.monotonic()` functions are high-resolution and are intended for timing and benchmarking. It is possible for the `time.perf_counter()` function to have higher resolution on some systems (e.g. use a different clock or sampling rate).

The `time.process_time()` function can be used if only the current process needs to be measured and the `time.thread_time()` for only the current threads. And these function should only be used if sleeps are to be ignored, which is probably desirable but could be confusing as it may differ from wall clock time.

Next, let's look at an example of benchmarking the same code with each time function.

8.2 Example of Comparing Time Measures

It may be interesting to compare each approach to timing the code all within the same program.

We can expect tiny differences between each time because the function calls will be sequential.

Nevertheless, we can expect large differences between some of the times because of the different clocks used for timing.

The comparison of all five timing methods is listed below.

```
# SuperFastPython.com
# example of timing a statement with each timing method
from time import time
from time import perf_counter
from time import monotonic
from time import process_time
from time import thread_time
# record start times
s1 = time()
s2 = perf_counter()
s3 = monotonic()
s4 = process_time()
s5 = thread_time()
# execute the statement
data = [i*i for i in range(100000000)]
# record end times
e1 = time()
e2 = perf_counter()
e3 = monotonic()
e4 = process_time()
e5 = thread_time()
# calculate the durations
d1 = e1 - s1
d2 = e2 - s2
```

```
d3 = e3 - s3
d4 = e4 - s4
d5 = e5 - s5
# report the durations
print(f'time:            {d1}')
print(f'perf_counter: {d2}')
print(f'monotonic:       {d3}')
print(f'process_time: {d4}')
print(f'thread_time:    {d5}')
```

Running the example we can see that the wall clock time report by
`time()` is very similar to the time reported by **perf_counter()** and
`monotonic()`

We can see that the **process_time()** and **thread_time()** are both
similar and both about 100 milliseconds shorter than the wall clock
times.

This may be because of some idle time during the execution of the
program that is excluded from the thread and process timers and
not from the other timers.

Alternately, it may be an artifact of the lower resolution (sampling
tick rate) of the clocks used by the thread and process times compared to the high-performance clock used by **perf_counter()** and
`monotonic()` and the higher resolution system clock.

I suspect the latter in this case.

Note, the results on your system may differ.

```
time:           5.1140899658203125
perf_counter: 5.113920567004243
monotonic:      5.113923772005364
process_time: 5.078392
thread_time:    5.078392597
```

8.3 `time()` Vs. `perf_counter()`

Perhaps the most common comparison we need to make is between the `time.time()` and `time.perf_counter()` functions.

The `time.time()` function is widely used for benchmarking, and as we have seen, it has some limitations.

The `time.perf_counter()` function is newer and is generally recommended, although few developers are aware of it, or of why we should be using it.

Let's take a closer look at a direct comparison of these two functions.

8.3.1 Similarities

The `time.time()` and `time.perf_counter()` functions are very similar, let's review some of the most important similarities.

- Both `time.time()` and `time.perf_counter()` functions are part of the `time` module. This module is concerned with time related functions.
- Both `time.time()` and `time.perf_counter()` report the current time of a clock. The `time.time()` function reports the time since epoch and the `time.perf_counter()` reports the time using a high-precision timer.
- Both `time.time()` and `time.perf_counter()` can be used for benchmarking. We can use either function to benchmark Python statements, functions, and entire programs.
- Both `time.time()` and `time.perf_counter()` are system-wide. This means that different programs calling the same functions will access consistent times.

8.3.2 Differences

The `time.time()` and `time.perf_counter()` are also quite different, let's review some of the most important differences.

- **Adjustable**. The clock used by `time.time()` is adjustable whereas the clock used by `time.perf_counter()` is not adjustable.

- **Monotonic.** The times returned by `time.time()` are not monotonic whereas the times returned by `time.perf_counter()` are monotonic.
- **Resolution.** The times returned by `time.time()` may have relatively lower precision whereas the times returned by `time.perf_counter()` may have higher relative precision.

Let's take a closer look at these differences in turn.

8.3.2.1 Adjustable

A clock is adjustable if it can be changed at any time.

The system clock is adjustable because it may be updated and changed to a new time.

> **adjustable:** `True` if the clock can be changed automatically (e.g. by an NTP daemon) or manually by the system administrator, `False` otherwise

– `time` – Time access and conversions.

This may be for many reasons, such as:

- Synchronization with a time server (called an NTP server).
- Adjustment for daylight savings (e.g. the start or end).
- Adjustment for leap seconds.
- Adjustment manually in system settings.

The `time.time()` function returns times based on the system clock. The system clock is adjustable. This means times have the potential to be very different from one call to `time.time()` to the next.

The clock used by the `time.perf_counter()` is not adjustable.

8.3.2.2 Monotonic

Monotonic is a mathematical term used to describe the values returned from a function.

A function is monotonic if the output values only ever increase with the increase of the input values.

> In mathematics, a monotonic function (or monotone function) is a function between ordered sets that preserves or reverses the given order.

– Monotonic function, Wikipedia.

A clock is monotonic if each time we retrieve a time it is greater than (or perhaps equal to) the previous time that was retrieved.

This is related to whether a clock is adjustable. For example, an adjustable clock is always a non-monotonic clock, and vice versa, a non-adjustable clock returns monotonic times.

> `monotonic`: `True` if the clock cannot go backward, `False` otherwise

– `time` – Time access and conversions.

The `time.perf_counter()` returns monotonic times, meaning that each time the function is called, a time is returned that is greater than or equal to the last time that was retrieved.

The `time.time()` function is not monotonic, meaning that it may report times in the past relative to times that have already been returned.

8.3.2.3   Resolution (Precision)

A clock's resolution refers to the smallest measurable increment in seconds.

A high-resolution clock is also interchangeably called a "high-precision" clock. Perhaps resolution refers to the sample rate of the clock and precision the nature of the numerical value (e.g. floating point precision). These concepts are related and it is confusing.

> In computer science, the precision of a numerical quantity is a measure of the detail in which the quantity is expressed. This is usually measured in bits, but sometimes

in decimal digits.

– Precision (computer science).

Nevertheless, for our purposes, a clock with a higher resolution/precision will be able to measure more ticks or change in a second than a lower resolution clock.

> The precision of the various real-time functions may be less than suggested by the units in which their value or argument is expressed.

– `time` – Time access and conversions.

The resolution of the `time.perf_counter()` function may be relatively higher than the resolution of clocks used by other time functions in the `time` module, such as the `time.time()` function.

> Return the value (in fractional seconds) of a performance counter, i.e. a clock with the highest available resolution to measure a short duration.

– `time` – Time access and conversions.

It is not guaranteed that the `time.perf_counter()` function will have higher resolution than time.time(), but if a clock with higher resolution (perhaps higher than the system clock) is available on the platform, then the `time.perf_counter()` function will make use of it.

8.3.3   Summary Of Differences

It may help to summarize the differences between `time.time()` and `time.perf_counter()`.

8.3.3.1   `time.time()`

- **Adjustable**, meaning the underlying clock may be changed at any time.
- **Non-monotonic**, meaning it may return times from the past.

- **Lower Resolution**, meaning it may use a clock with fewer ticks per time interval than other clocks.

8.3.3.2 time.perf_counter()

- **Non-adjustable**, meaning the underlying clock cannot be changed.
- **Monotonic**, meaning that each time returned will always be equal or greater than the last time returned.
- **Higher Resolution**, meaning it may use a clock with more ticks per time interval than other clocks.

8.4 monotonic() Vs. perf_counter()

The choice between time.monotonic() and time.perf_counter() is less contested.

Generally, both time.perf_counter() and time.monotonic() are functions provided by Python's time module for measuring time intervals and durations.

They are both monotonic and non-adjustable. The question between these two functions is to why bother use one over the other?

Importantly, they serve slightly different purposes and have distinct characteristics:

1. Purpose:

- time.perf_counter(): This function returns a clock with the highest available resolution to measure a monotonic, continuous, and linearly increasing time. It's well-suited for benchmarking, profiling, and measuring short durations with high precision. It includes time intervals during which the system is sleeping or in an idle state.
- time.monotonic(): This function also returns a monotonic clock, but it doesn't guarantee high resolution. Its primary purpose is to measure time intervals in a way that's immune to system clock adjustments and provides a reliable way to

measure real-world time spans. It excludes time intervals when the system is sleeping or in an idle state.

2. Accuracy and Resolution:

- `time.perf_counter()`: This function provides the highest resolution available from the system's hardware clock. It's suitable for measuring very short durations and is highly accurate for benchmarking and profiling.
- `time.monotonic()`: While it's also monotonic, the resolution of `time.monotonic()` might be lower than that of `time.perf_counter()`. It focuses more on providing a reliable representation of time intervals while being immune to system clock changes.

3. Use Cases:

- `time.perf_counter()`: Best suited for benchmarking, performance measurement, profiling, and any scenario where high-resolution timing is essential.
- `time.monotonic()`: Ideal for measuring real-world time intervals, intervals between events, and any situation where consistency is important.

If we need high-resolution timing for short durations and accurate performance measurements, the `time.perf_counter()` function is appropriate.

8.5 General Recommendations

Now that we have compared the 5 techniques for measuring time using the `time` module, let's consider some general recommendations about when to use each function.

8.5.1 Time Functions For Benchmarking

When benchmarking the execution time of code, use the `time.perf_counter()` function.

This is because:

- It uses the clock available with the highest precision.
- It is monotonic.
- It is not adjustable.

A fallback is the `time.monotonic()` function for similar reasons.

If just need to profile the performance of Python processes or threads separately and things are getting messy with `time.perf_counter()`, then consider `time.process_time()` and `time.thread_time()` functions to constrain the clock to a given process or thread.

8.5.2 Time Functions For Waiting

When waiting for a future condition in Python code, such as a timeout or time limit, use the `time.monotonic()` function.

This is because:

- It is monotonic.
- It is not adjustable.

It may also be slightly more efficient if it uses a clock with less precision than the `time.perf_counter()` function. Less precision is almost always fine for normal waiting code.

8.5.3 Time Functions In Legacy Code

The standard way to benchmark Python code for a long time was via the `time.time()` function.

Legacy code will use the `time.time()` function and we may need to continue to use it for this reason.

Additionally, use `time.time()` to achieve consistency with other system tools that also use time since epoch.

8.6   Further Reading

This section lists helpful additional resources on the topic.

8.6.1   References

- Epoch (computing), Wikipedia.
  https://en.wikipedia.org/wiki/Epoch_(computing)
- time (Unix), Wikipedia.
  https://en.wikipedia.org/wiki/Time_(Unix)
- Monotonic function, Wikipedia.
  https://en.wikipedia.org/wiki/Monotonic_function
- Precision (computer science).
  https://en.wikipedia.org/wiki/Precision_(computer_science)

8.6.2   APIs

- `time` – Time access and conversions.
  https://docs.python.org/3/library/time.html
- `timeit` – Measure execution time of small code snippets.
  https://docs.python.org/3/library/timeit.html
- What's New In Python 3.3.
  https://docs.python.org/3/whatsnew/3.3.html
- PEP 418 – Add monotonic time, performance counter, and
  process time functions.
  https://peps.python.org/pep-0418/

8.7   Takeaways

You now know how to time the execution of Python code using a
suite of different techniques.

Specifically, you know:

- How the details of each of the 5 time functions compare, such
  as adjustable, monotonic, and resolution.
- How to compare the `time.time()` and `time.perf_counter()`
  functions and when to use each.

- How to choose time functions for benchmarking and other tasks such as waiting and timeouts.

8.7.1 Next

In the next tutorial, we will explore best practices when benchmarking execution time.

Part III

Benchmarking Best Practices

Measuring execution time is just the first step in benchmarking.

There are other considerations before we can present results or make decisions, such as:

- Calculating metrics that compare one measure to another.
- Repeating benchmarks many times and reporting stable summary statistics.
- Selecting the appropriate numerical precision and units of measure for results.

The chapters in this section take a moment to consider these aspects and the best practices to follow after benchmark results have been collected.

Chapter 9

Benchmark Metrics

You can calculate benchmark metrics like the difference and the speedup in order to compare the performance improvements of different versions of a program.

In this tutorial, you will discover how to calculate metrics to compare the benchmark performance of programs in Python.

After completing this tutorial, you will know:

- How to calculate and compare the difference in execution time.
- How to calculate and compare the speedup factor in execution time.
- How to report and interpret the difference and speedup factors when benchmarking.

Let's get started.

9.1 Compare Benchmark Results

It is good practice to develop a simple and working version of a program before making changes.

This is to ensure the testability and correctness of the code before adding complexity.

For example, we may:

- Develop a sequential version of a program before making it concurrent.
- Develop a simple and slow version before optimizing performance.

Often, our goal is to improve the performance of a program by reducing the execution runtime of the program.

This requires first that the initial or slow version of the program be benchmarked. The time taken to run the this version of the program provides a baseline of comparison that all updated versions of the program must improve upon, e.g. run in a shorter overall execution time.

The next step is to benchmark the new or changed versions of the program. This assumes that we have candidate ideas as to how to improve performance, such as:

- Replacing function calls.
- Using alternative mathematical operators.
- Adding threads or processes for concurrent execution.

Finally, the performance of the two versions can be compared. But how?

There are many ways we could compare two or more sets of benchmark results.

What are the best ways to compare the performance of our programs?

9.2   How To Calculate Benchmark Metrics

There are two metrics that we can use to directly compare benchmark results , they are:

1. Difference
2. Speedup (factor)

Let's take a closer look at each in turn.

9.2.1   How To Calculate Benchmark Difference

The **difference metric** refers to the benchmark of the updated (faster) program subtracted from the benchmark of the initial or baseline (slow) version of the program.

The result indicates how much faster (or slower) the new version of the program is compared to the initial version.

It is calculated as follows:

- difference = baseline_duration - updated_duration

The result should be above zero, indicating an improvement in the performance of the updated version over the baseline version of the program.

Once calculated, we can then report the result, for example:

- *The updated version is [difference] seconds faster than the base-line version*

9.2.1.1   What If The Difference Is Zero?

If the difference is zero, or close to zero, then we can say that the benchmark performance of the program is equal or nearly equal.

That there is no execution time performance benefit from the updated version.

9.2.1.2   What If The Difference Is Negative?

The difference result can be negative.

This means that the updated version takes longer to execute than the baseline version.

In this case, the updated version has a worse performance benchmark than the baseline version performance benchmark.

When reporting this result, we can remove the negative sign from the result and change "faster" to "slower" in the summary.

For example:

- *The updated version is [difference] seconds slower than the baseline version*

9.2.2 How To Calculate Benchmark Speedup

We can use the benchmark scores for the baseline and updated programs to calculate the speedup metric.

That is, what is the speedup of the updated version of the program compared to the baseline version of the program?

> In computer architecture, speedup is a number that measures the relative performance of two systems processing the same problem. More technically, it is the improvement in speed of execution of a task executed on two similar architectures with different resources.

– Speedup, Wikipedia.

The speedup, which is more formally called the "speedup factor", is calculated as the performance benchmark of the baseline version of the program divided by the performance benchmark for the updated version of the program.

It is calculated as follows:

- speedup_factor $= \frac{\text{baseline\_duration}}{\text{updated\_duration}}$

The result should be above one, indicating an improvement in the performance of the updated version over the baseline version of the program.

The result is not a time in seconds. It is a factor. It is sometimes referred to as the "latency", as in "the speedup in latency" when measuring the time taken for a task or program.

Once calculated, we can report the speedup for the updated version as follows:

- *The updated version has a [speedup_factor]x speedup over the baseline version*

Or perhaps:

- *The updated version is [speedup_factor] times faster than the baseline version*

9.2.2.1 What If The Speedup Is 1?

If the speedup is one or close to one, then it suggests that the performance of the baseline and updated versions of the program are equivalent or nearly equivalent.

It suggests that there is no execution time performance benefit in adopting the updated version of the program over the baseline version.

9.2.2.2 What If The Speedup Is Less Than 1?

The speedup could be less than one, e.g. 0.5.

This means that the updated version does not offer a speedup over the baseline version of the program.

In this case, the terms in the calculation could be switched.

For example:

- speedup_factor $= \frac{\text{updated\_duration}}{\text{baseline\_duration}}$

The way the result is reported can then be changed to highlight that the updated version is slower than the baseline version.

For example:

- *The updated version has a [speedup_factor]x slowdown over the baseline version*

Or perhaps:

- *The updated version is [speedup_factor] times slower than the baseline version*

Now that we know how to calculate performance benchmarks, let's look at some worked examples.

9.3   Example Of Benchmarking Sequential Vs. Concurrent

Before calculating performance benchmarks for comparison, we need to benchmark two versions of a program.

In this example we will develop a sequential version of a program that executes multiple tasks and benchmark it. We will then update the program to be faster by using concurrency, then benchmark the new version.

These benchmarks will then be used as a basis for calculating metrics for comparison in subsequent sections.

9.3.1   Benchmarking Sequential Tasks

We can develop a program to sequentially execute tasks.

Firstly, we will define a task that takes an argument and then blocks for one second to simulate effort.

```
# task function
def task(data):
    # block for a moment to simulate work
    sleep(1)
```

We will hen execute 20 of these tasks sequentially, one-by-one.

```
# do all the work
def main():
    # execute many tasks concurrently
    for i in range(20):
        task(i)
```

Because there are 20 tasks and each task takes 1 second, then we expect the program to complete in about 20 seconds.

Finally, we will benchmark the execution time of the program manually using the `time.perf_counter()` function.

```python
# protect the entry point
if __name__ == '__main__':
    # record start time
    time_start = perf_counter()
    # call benchmark code
    main()
    # calculate the duration
    time_duration = perf_counter() - time_start
    # report the duration
    print(f'Took {time_duration:.3f} seconds')
```

Tying this together, the complete example is listed below.

```python
# SuperFastPython.com
# example of a program that executes tasks sequentially
from time import perf_counter
from time import sleep

# task function
def task(data):
    # block for a moment to simulate work
    sleep(1)

# do all the work
def main():
    # execute many tasks concurrently
    for i in range(20):
        task(i)

# protect the entry point
if __name__ == '__main__':
    # record start time
    time_start = perf_counter()
```

```
# call benchmark code
main()
# calculate the duration
time_duration = perf_counter() - time_start
# report the duration
print(f'Took {time_duration:.3f} seconds')
```

Running the program executes all 20 tasks sequentially in a loop.

Finally, the benchmark execution time is reported.

As expected, the program takes about 20 seconds to complete.

Note, the results on your system may differ.

```
Took 20.053 seconds
```

Next, let's look at how we can update the program to use concurrency and benchmark the performance.

9.3.2   Benchmarking Concurrent Tasks

We can update the example to execute the tasks concurrently.

This can be achieved using the `ThreadPoolExecutor` with one worker per task, and issuing all tasks at once for concurrent execution.

For example:

```
...
# create the thread pool
n = 20
with ThreadPoolExecutor(n_tasks) as tpe:
    # issue all tasks
    _ = [tpe.submit(task, i) for i in range(n)]
# wait for all tasks to complete
```

The expectation is that because all 20 tasks are to be executed concurrently, the overall execution time of the program should drop to about one second, the duration of one task.

Tying this together, the complete example is listed below.

```python
# SuperFastPython.com
# example of a program that executes tasks concurrently
from time import perf_counter
from time import sleep
from concurrent.futures import ThreadPoolExecutor

# task function
def task(data):
    # block for a moment to simulate work
    sleep(1)

# do all the work
def main():
    # create the thread pool
    n = 20
    with ThreadPoolExecutor(n) as tpe:
        # issue all tasks
        _ = [tpe.submit(task, i) for i in range(n)]
    # wait for all tasks to complete

# protect the entry point
if __name__ == '__main__':
    # record start time
    time_start = perf_counter()
    # call benchmark code
    main()
    # calculate the duration
    time_duration = perf_counter() - time_start
    # report the duration
    print(f'Took {time_duration:.3f} seconds')
```

Running the program executes all 20 tasks concurrently in the thread pool.

Finally, the benchmark execution time is reported.

As expected, the program takes about 1 second to complete.

Note, the results on your system may differ.

`Took 1.006 seconds`

Next, let's review the benchmark results.

9.3.3   Benchmark Results

Before calculating metrics, it is important to review the benchmark results.

The table below summarizes each program and lists the benchmark execution time in seconds.

Method	Result (sec)
Sequential	20.053
Concurrent	1.006

Looking at the raw benchmark results, we can see that obviously, one program is much faster than the other.

But how much faster and how can we report this result?

Next, let's look at how we can calculate performance benchmark metrics for reporting.

9.4   Example Of Calculating Difference

We can explore how to calculate the difference metric using the real execution time performance benchmark results from the previous section.

Recall, the calculation for the difference metric is as follows:

- difference = sequential_duration - concurrent_duration

We can then plug in the execution time results from our sequential and concurrent benchmarks and calculate the difference.

- difference = 20.053 - 1.006

- difference = 19.047

We can then report the result using our template, for example:

- *The concurrent version is 19.047 seconds faster than the sequential version*

It is also a good idea to put the result in a table, as it is likely we will benchmark many concurrent variations of the original program (e.g. processes, threads, asyncio, varied number of workers, etc.).

Method	Difference (sec)
Sequential	n/a
Concurrent	19.047

Next, let's look at how we might calculate the speedup metric.

9.5 Example Of Calculating Speedup

We can explore how to calculate the speedup metric using the real execution time performance benchmark results from the previous section.

Recall, the calculation for the speedup metric is as follows:

- speedup_factor $= \frac{\text{sequential\_duration}}{\text{concurrent\_duration}}$

We can then plug in the execution time results from our sequential and concurrent benchmarks and calculate the difference.

- speedup_factor $= \frac{20.053}{1.006}$
- speedup_factor $= 19.933$

We can then report the result using our template, for example:

- *The concurrent version has a 19.933x speedup over the sequential version*

Or perhaps:

- *The concurrent version is 19.933 times faster than the sequential version*

It is also a good idea to put the result in a table, as it is likely we will benchmark many concurrent variations of the original program.

Method	Speedup (multiple)
Sequential	n/a
Concurrent	19.933x

9.6   Further Reading

This section lists helpful additional resources on the topic.

- Percentage increase and decrease, Wikipedia.
  https://en.wikipedia.org/wiki/Percentage
- Speedup, Wikipedia.
  https://en.wikipedia.org/wiki/Speedup
- `time` – Time access and conversions.
  https://docs.python.org/3/library/time.html
- `concurrent.futures` – Launching parallel tasks.
  https://docs.python.org/3/library/concurrent.futures.html

9.7   Takeaways

You now know how to calculate metrics to compare the benchmark performance of baseline versus updated programs in Python.

Specifically, you know:

- How to calculate and compare the difference in execution time.
- How to calculate and compare the speedup factor in execution time.
- How to report and interpret the difference and speedup factors when benchmarking.

9.7.1 Next

In the next tutorial, we will explore the importance of repeating benchmark tests and using summary statistics.

Chapter 10

Benchmark Repetition

You can improve the benchmark estimate by repeating a benchmark many times and reporting the average score.

Each time a benchmark is performed, a different result will be reported. This is for many reasons such as other activity in the operating system, external dependencies, hardware behavior, and more. The result is an estimate of the performance of a program with added random statistical noise.

We can counter the statistical noise in single benchmark results by repeating a benchmark many times and averaging the result, canceling out a lot of the variation. This will give a more stable estimate of performance, an estimate that if repeated would show a closer or nearly identical result.

In this tutorial, you will discover how to develop stable benchmark measures in Python.

After completing this tutorial, you will know:

- Why benchmark measures differ each time they are reported.
- How repetition and summary statistics can be used to gather and report stable benchmark results.
- How to implement repeated benchmark tests and correctly report results.

Let's get started.

10.1 Benchmark Results Differ Every Time

A problem with benchmarking Python code is that we will get a different benchmark result every time.

For example, we can use functions like `time.time()` or `time.perf_counter()` to record a start time before a block of code, and an end time after the target code and calculate and report the difference between the two times.

Repeating this simple benchmark more than once will give different results.

Which value should we report as the benchmark score?

- The first time reported?
- The best or lowest time?
- The worst case or largest time?

How do we handle the case that benchmark results differ from one run to the next?

Next, let's consider why benchmark execution times vary.

10.1.1 Why Do Execution Times Vary

Execution time results can differ in each run due to various factors and sources of variability.

Understanding these factors is crucial for accurate performance analysis.

Some common reasons why execution time results can vary from run to run include:

1. **Operating System Activity**: Background processes and system activity can affect the execution of our code. The

operating system may allocate or deallocate resources, causing variations in execution time.

2. **CPU Load**: The CPU may be shared with other processes and tasks running on the system. CPU load fluctuations can impact how quickly our code is processed.

3. **Memory Usage**: Changes in memory usage, such as garbage collection or memory swapping, can affect the execution of code, especially if it leads to cache misses or increased paging.

4. **Concurrency**: On multi-core systems, the scheduling and interaction of threads or processes (other than those in our program) can introduce variability in execution times. Competition for CPU resources can result in varying execution speeds.

5. **External Dependencies**: Code that relies on external services or data sources, such as network requests or database queries, can experience variable execution times due to network latency or resource availability.

6. **Compiler Optimizations**: Some Python interpreters may apply optimizations during code execution. These optimizations can affect the speed at which code is executed and may not be consistent across runs.

7. **Caching**: The availability and state of CPU caches and memory hierarchies can impact the execution speed. Caching effects can vary from run to run.

8. **Randomness**: Code that involves random number generation, such as simulations or games, can produce different results each time it runs. This is expected behavior and not necessarily an issue.

9. **CPU Frequency Scaling**: Some CPUs support dynamic frequency scaling, which adjusts the CPU clock speed based on demand. This can lead to variations in execution speed.

10. **Resource Contention**: Resource contention, such as disk or network I/O, can introduce delays and affect execution times if multiple processes or threads compete for the same resources.

The system is never the same from moment to moment.

We must expect benchmark results to vary.

Therefore, we need to manage or control for the variability in benchmark results.

Next, let's consider the problems that varying benchmark results introduce.

10.1.2   The Problem With Benchmark Results That Vary

Using and reporting benchmark results from a single run can lead to several issues and inaccuracies in performance analysis.

This can lead to problems, such as:

1. **Unreliable Data**: A single benchmark run can be highly susceptible to variations caused by factors like background processes, CPU load, and random fluctuations. Relying on a single run may result in unreliable and misleading performance data.
2. **Inaccurate Assessment**: Without multiple runs and averaging, it's challenging to accurately assess the true performance characteristics of code. Reported results may not reflect the code's typical behavior.
3. **Misleading Optimization Decisions**: Making optimization decisions based on a single run can be risky. A minor change in external conditions during that run can lead to the incorrect perception that an optimization is effective or ineffective.
4. **Failure to Identify Regressions**: When comparing different code versions or implementations, a single-run approach might not detect performance regressions or improvements accurately. A single lucky or unlucky run can skew the comparison.
5. **Lack of Confidence**: Stakeholders, including developers and project managers, may lack confidence in performance claims based on a single run. They may question the validity of the results and the reliability of optimizations.

10.2 Use Repetition To Fairly Estimate Performance

We can use simple statistics to develop a stable benchmark result.

This can be achieved by repeating a given benchmark more than once and calculating the average.

From a statistical perspective, there is a true but unknown underlying benchmark time. Each time we perform a benchmark and collect a benchmark time, we are estimating the true but unknown benchmark time, but the problem is the estimate has statistical noise added to it, because of the reasons we discussed above.

Therefore, to overcome the statistical noise, we can draw many samples of the benchmark time by repeating the benchmark many times.

Calculating a summary statistic such as the minimum, or average of these samples will get much closer to the true unknown underlying benchmark time. The random statistical noise will cancel out and we will be left with a much closer approximation of the true benchmark time.

10.2.1 The Procedure for Repeated Benchmarking

The old procedure is as follows:

1. Determine the code to benchmark and instrument with an appropriate time measure.
2. Benchmark the code and report the score.

We know that this is not good enough as we will report a different score every time the benchmark is performed.

Therefore, the better procedure for repeating a benchmark and reporting the average is as follows:

1. Determine the code to benchmark and instrument with an appropriate time measure.
2. Loop a number of times.
    1. Benchmark the code.
    2. Record the score.
3. Calculate and report the average of the scores.

This will give a better estimate of the benchmark.

10.2.2   Why Repeat a Benchmark Many Times

Repeating a code benchmark many times and reporting the average is a common practice in performance analysis for several reasons:

1. **Statistical Significance**: A single measurement of code execution time can be subject to random variations caused by factors like system load, background processes, and CPU fluctuations. Repeating the benchmark multiple times helps reduce the impact of these variations and provides a more representative sample of performance data.
2. **Stability Assessment**: By taking the average of multiple runs, we can assess the stability of our code's performance. If there is significant variability in execution times, it may indicate underlying issues that need to be addressed.
3. **Outlier Detection**: Repeating benchmarks allows us to identify and discard outliers, which are unusually slow or fast measurements that can skew the results. Outliers can be caused by various factors, such as context switches, I/O delays, or CPU spikes.
4. **Minimizing Noise**: Benchmarks can be affected by noise introduced by the operating system or other background processes. Averaging multiple runs helps minimize the impact of this noise, providing a more accurate measurement of the code's performance.
5. **Meaningful Comparison**: When comparing the performance of different code implementations or optimizations, taking the average of multiple runs ensures that the comparison is based on stable and reliable data, making the results more meaningful.

6. **Response to Variability**: In real-world applications, code performance can vary due to changing inputs or system conditions. Repeating benchmarks allows us to observe how our code's performance responds to such variability and whether it remains within acceptable bounds.

7. **Validating Changes**: When making code changes or optimizations, repeating benchmarks before and after the changes can help us assess the impact of those changes accurately. Averaging ensures that any improvements or regressions are not due to random fluctuations.

8. **Fair Assessment**: Averaging provides a fairer representation of the code's performance because it accounts for the variability in execution time that may occur during different runs.

Repeating a code benchmark multiple times and reporting the average is essential for obtaining accurate, reliable, and statistically significant performance measurements.

10.2.3 How Many Times To Repeat The Benchmark

The result of the procedure will be a stable estimate of the execution time of the target code.

Stable means that we could repeat the same procedure on the same code and on the same computer system at a later date and get an estimate of the execution time that is close to the same value, much closer than two individual runs.

Two average execution times will not be identical, there will be small differences and there always will be. This is the nature of statistical measurements. The difference accounts for statistical noise that we are unable to remove from the estimate. If there was no statistical noise, we would not need to estimate in the first place, one run and measurement would be sufficient.

We can improve the estimate of the performance, which will reduce the difference between two runs of the procedure.

This can be achieved by increasing the number of samples, e.g. the number of repetitions of the benchmark.

How many repetitions are needed?

- One repetition is not sufficient, we now know this.
- A minimum number of repetitions is 3.
- A reasonable number of repetitions is 10.
- A good number of repetitions is 30.
- A great number of repetitions is 100 or 1,000, maybe even 1,000,000.

More than 100 or 1,000 repetitions quickly reaches a point of diminishing returns, depending on the code that is being benchmarked.

Generally, the number of repetitions comes down to how long we can afford to wait.

Few repetitions are used with slower code, more repetitions are used with faster code.

10.3 How To Calculate The Average Benchmark Score

The first step is to collect multiple individual benchmark scores.

These can be collected in a list.

For example, if we had a function named `benchmark()` that performed a single benchmark of the target code and returned a time in seconds, we could call this many times and store the results in a list.

...
```
# the number of times to repeat the benchmark
n_repeats = 30
# collect a list of benchmark scores
all_times = [benchmark() _ for i in range(n_repeats)]
```

Or, we might use a for loop and report each individual score along the way to show progress.

I like this approach, it might look as follows:

```
...
# the number of times to repeat the benchmark
n_repeats = 30
# benchmark results
all_times = list()
# repeat benchmark may times
for i in range(n_repeats):
    # calculate the duration
    time_duration = benchmark()
    # report the duration
    print(f'>trial {i} took {time_duration} seconds')
    # store the result
    all_times.append(time_duration)
```

The average is also referred to by the technical name *arithmetic mean* and is calculated as the sum of all times divided by the number of times that were collected.

> In mathematics and statistics, the arithmetic mean, arithmetic average, or just the mean or average (when the context is clear) is the sum of a collection of numbers divided by the count of numbers in the collection.

– Arithmetic mean, Wikipedia.

For example:

- average $= \frac{\text{sum of all scores}}{\text{number of scores collected}}$

In code, we can use the built-in **sum()** function, for example:

```
...
# calculate the average duration
time_avg = sum(all_times) / repeats
# report the average time
print(f'Took {time_avg} seconds on average')
```

We can also calculate the average using the **statistics.mean()** function.

For example:

```
...
# calculate the mean score
time_avg = statistics.mean(all_times)
```

I prefer to calculate the mean myself instead of using the `statistics.mean()` function as it does not require any additional imports.

When we report the score, we must indicate that it is an average rather than a single estimate of performance.

For example:

```
...
Took 2.3 seconds on average
```

It might also be a good idea to report the standard deviation.

Recall the mean is the expected value or middle of a normal (bell curve) distribution. The standard deviation is the average spread in the same sample distribution.

> In statistics, the standard deviation is a measure of the amount of variation or dispersion of a set of values. A low standard deviation indicates that the values tend to be close to the mean (also called the expected value) of the set, while a high standard deviation indicates that the values are spread out over a wider range.

– Standard deviation, Wikipedia.

If we have both the mean and the standard deviation values, we can reconstruct the sample distribution. This is helpful when reporting results formally, such as in a report or research context. Someone familiar with statistics can then use statistical tools to compare distributions directly (e.g. benchmarks with and without a change) and report the statistical significance of the results (e.g. did the change really make a difference). This is out of the scope of this tutorial.

Don't calculate the standard deviation manually. There are a few ways to calculate it and we may use the wrong one (e.g. population vs. sample standard deviation). Instead, we can use the `statistics.stdev()` function to calculate the standard deviation of the sample.

For example:

```
...
# calculate the standard deviation
time_stdv = statistics.stdev(all_times)
```

We can report the mean and standard deviation together:

```
...
Took 2.3 seconds on average (std=0.1)
```

For completeness, we can also report the number of benchmark repetitions that were sampled, reported as "n".

For example:

```
...
Took 2.3 seconds on average (stdev=0.1, n=10)
```

In most cases, reporting the average time is sufficient in order to make decisions by ourselves.

I would recommend including the standard deviation (stdev) and number of repetitions (n) only when reporting results formally, or when someone else also needs to review the results to help make a decision.

Now that we know how to calculate the average benchmark score, let's look at some worked examples.

10.4 Example Of Variable Benchmark Results

Before we look at how to repeat a benchmark and calculate the average score, let's confirm that performing the same single benchmark many times results in a different score each time.

In this case, we will define a task that creates a list of squared integers. We will then benchmark this function and report the duration in seconds. We will record the time before and after the target code using the `time.perf_counter()` function.

Firstly, we can define a `task()` function that performs the CPU-intensive task of creating a list of 100 million squared integers in a list comprehension.

```
# function to benchmark
def task():
    # create a large list
    data = [i*i for i in range(100000000)]
```

Next, we can define a `benchmark()` function that records the start time, calls the `task()` function, records the end time, and calculates and reports the overall duration in seconds.

```
# benchmark the task() function
def benchmark():
    # record start time
    time_start = perf_counter()
    # execute the function
    task()
    # record end time
    time_end = perf_counter()
    # calculate the duration
    time_duration = time_end - time_start
    # report the duration
    print(f'Took {time_duration:.3f} seconds')
```

The benchmarking of the target `task()` function is performed in a standalone function named `benchmark()`. We will call this function multiple times, and a benchmark score will be reported each time.

```
...
# repeat the same benchmark a few times
benchmark()
benchmark()
benchmark()
```

Tying this together, the complete example is listed below.

```python
# SuperFastPython.com
# example a variability in benchmark results
from time import perf_counter

# function to benchmark
def task():
    # create a large list
    data = [i*i for i in range(100000000)]

# benchmark the task() function
def benchmark():
    # record start time
    time_start = perf_counter()
    # execute the function
    task()
    # record end time
    time_end = perf_counter()
    # calculate the duration
    time_duration = time_end - time_start
    # report the duration
    print(f'Took {time_duration:.3f} seconds')

# repeat the same benchmark a few times
benchmark()
benchmark()
benchmark()
```

Running the example benchmarks the same `task()` function three times.

In this case, we can see that each time the `task()` function is benchmarked, we get a different score.

The results are truncated to 3 decimal places to keep things simple. If we allowed full double floating-point precision and ran the same benchmark thousands of times, we would likely get thousands of different benchmark scores.

The reason for the difference is because of random statistical noise in the estimate of the benchmark time.

Note, the results on your system may differ.

This highlights that we can expect to get a different benchmark result every time we execute a single benchmark.

```
Took 6.138 seconds
Took 5.920 seconds
Took 5.904 seconds
```

Next, let's explore how we can make the benchmark more stable by repeating it many times and reporting the average.

10.5   Example Of Average Benchmark Results

We can explore how to repeat a benchmark many times and report the average result.

In this case, we can update the above example to perform the same benchmark many times, collect the results, and report the average.

Firstly, we can update the `benchmark()` function to return the duration rather than report it.

```
# benchmark the task() function
def benchmark():
    # record start time
    time_start = perf_counter()
    # execute the function
    task()
    # record end time
    time_end = perf_counter()
    # calculate the duration
    time_duration = time_end - time_start
    # return the duration
    return time_duration
```

Next, we can define a new function `repeat_benchmark()` that defines the number of repeats and a list for storing all duration times.

It then loops and calls the `benchmark()` function many times and stores each result. It then calculates the average of all duration times and reports the average.

```python
# repeat a benchmark
def repeat_benchmark():
    # define the number of repeats
    n_repeats = 30
    # list for storing all results
    all_times = list()
    # repeat benchmark may times
    for i in range(n_repeats):
        # benchmark and retrieve the duration
        time_duration = benchmark()
        # report the duration
        print(f'>{i} took {time_duration:.3f} seconds')
        # store the result
        all_times.append(time_duration)
    # calculate the average duration
    time_avg = sum(all_times) / n_repeats
    # report the average time
    print(f'Took {time_avg:.3f} seconds on average')
```

We can then call this function to perform the repeated benchmark of the `task()` function and calculate a stable estimate of the function's performance.

```python
...
# execute a repeated benchmark
repeat_benchmark()
```

Tying this together, the complete example is listed below.

```python
# SuperFastPython.com
# example a stable benchmark results
from time import perf_counter
```

```python
# function to benchmark
def task():
    # create a large list
    data = [i*i for i in range(100000000)]

# benchmark the task() function
def benchmark():
    # record start time
    time_start = perf_counter()
    # execute the function
    task()
    # record end time
    time_end = perf_counter()
    # calculate the duration
    time_duration = time_end - time_start
    # return the duration
    return time_duration

# repeat a benchmark
def repeat_benchmark():
    # define the number of repeats
    n_repeats = 30
    # list for storing all results
    all_times = list()
    # repeat benchmark may times
    for i in range(n_repeats):
        # benchmark and retrieve the duration
        time_duration = benchmark()
        # report the duration
        print(f'>{i} took {time_duration:.3f} seconds')
        # store the result
        all_times.append(time_duration)
    # calculate the average duration
    time_avg = sum(all_times) / n_repeats
    # report the average time
    print(f'Took {time_avg:.3f} seconds on average')
```

```
# execute a repeated benchmark
repeat_benchmark()
```

Running the example benchmarks the `task()` function 30 times and reports the average execution time.

Helpfully, the estimated performance is reported in each iteration, showing how the estimated time of the `task()` function varies each time the `benchmark()` function is run.

In this case, the average duration is reported as 5.997 seconds.

Note, the results on your system may differ.

```
>0 took 5.999 seconds
>1 took 6.250 seconds
>2 took 6.115 seconds
>3 took 6.057 seconds
>4 took 6.132 seconds
>5 took 6.155 seconds
>6 took 6.106 seconds
>7 took 6.119 seconds
>8 took 5.938 seconds
>9 took 5.949 seconds
>10 took 5.935 seconds
>11 took 5.912 seconds
>12 took 6.102 seconds
>13 took 6.015 seconds
>14 took 5.980 seconds
>15 took 5.905 seconds
>16 took 5.899 seconds
>17 took 5.916 seconds
>18 took 5.912 seconds
>19 took 5.990 seconds
>20 took 5.966 seconds
>21 took 5.933 seconds
>22 took 6.043 seconds
>23 took 6.008 seconds
```

```
>24 took 5.919 seconds
>25 took 5.897 seconds
>26 took 5.931 seconds
>27 took 5.919 seconds
>28 took 5.953 seconds
>29 took 5.954 seconds
Took 5.997 seconds on average
```

This result is more stable than a single run of the `benchmark()` function.

We can demonstrate this.

Re-run the entire program and note the result.

In this case, the result is 5.994 seconds. This is very close to the 5.997 seconds reported in the previous run, showing the stability of the procedure for the `task()` function.

```
...
>25 took 5.965 seconds
>26 took 5.951 seconds
>27 took 5.966 seconds
>28 took 5.947 seconds
>29 took 6.036 seconds
Took 5.994 seconds on average
```

We could achieve even more stability by increasing the number of repeats from 30 to 100 and perhaps increasing the precision of the average result from 3 decimal places to 6 to look for any differences.

10.6   Further Reading

This section lists helpful additional resources on the topic.

- Arithmetic mean, Wikipedia.
  https://en.wikipedia.org/wiki/Arithmetic_mean
- Standard deviation, Wikipedia.
  https://en.wikipedia.org/wiki/Standard_deviation

- `statistics` – Mathematical statistics functions.
  https://docs.python.org/3/library/statistics.html
- `time` – Time access and conversions.
  https://docs.python.org/3/library/time.html

10.7   Takeaways

You now know how to develop stable benchmark measures in Python.

Specifically, you know:

- Why benchmark measures differ each time they are reported.
- How repetition and summary statistics can be used to gather and report stable benchmark results.
- How to implement repeated benchmark tests and correctly report results.

10.7.1   Next

In the next tutorial, we will explore best practices when reporting benchmark precision and units of measure.

Chapter 11

Benchmark Reporting

You can carefully choose the level of precision and units of measure when presenting benchmark results.

These are the two main areas when presenting benchmark results that can introduce confusion and unnecessary cognitive load when attempting to interpret, analyze, and compare results.

Getting precision and units of measure correct will go a long way to ensuring execution time benchmark results are presented well.

In this tutorial, you will discover helpful tips to consider when presenting execution time benchmark results.

After completing this tutorial, you will know:

- Why collecting benchmark results is one step in a broader project.
- How to consider the precision when presenting benchmark results.
- How to consider the units of measure when presenting benchmark results.

Let's get started.

11.1   Need To Present Benchmark Results

Recording benchmark results is the first step.

Typically, the second step involves presenting the results before a decision can be made to explore changes to the system.

We may need to report benchmark results to many people such as:

- A team lead or manager.
- Peer developers in the same team.
- Project stakeholders.

Presenting raw results can be a problem.

This is typically for two main reasons:

1. The precision of the benchmark results is often high, leading to confusion.
2. The units of measure may be missing or limited to the default of seconds, which may not be appropriate.

We can focus on considerations when presenting results in these two areas, namely precision of measure and units of measure.

Let's take a close look at each in turn.

11.2   Tips For Benchmark Measure Precision

The precision of the result refers to the number of decimal places used to present results.

The default for benchmark results will be full double floating point precision, which is 16 decimal places on most platforms.

This can be confusing to managers, fellow developers, and stakeholders alike.

Below are some tips with regard to measurement precision when presenting results.

11.2.1 Tip 01: Don't Report Too Much Precision

When presenting a measure, don't include too much precision.

Limit the precision to make a main point, such as the level of precision that highlights the main difference between measures.

Precision can be limited in many ways, such as by truncation and rounding.

Precision can also be adjusted by changing the unit of measure so that the main difference between measures appears before the decimal point.

11.2.2 Tip 02: Don't Report Too Little Precision

A danger when limiting precision is limiting it too much.

We must give some indication that additional precision is available, meaning we probably should not round results to integer values, at least not without good reason.

A balance must be struck between clearly showing the main focus of the measure, e.g. the difference between different measure values, and the fact that additional precision is available but was limited for presentation reasons.

11.2.3 Tip 03: Be Consistent

We may present many measures within one report and across reports.

Ensure that the presentation of results is consistent. That all measures are reported using the same level of precision, e.g. three decimal places.

This consistency will allow values to be compared directly without additional cognitive load.

This may include zero padding the precision to ensure that numbers are right-aligned in a table or column.

11.2.4   Tip 04: Prefer to Truncate Over Round

Rounding is an algorithm that involves replacing a number with an approximated number.

> Rounding means replacing a number with an approximate value that has a shorter, simpler, or more explicit representation.

– Rounding, Wikipedia.

There are many algorithms available and variations such as taking the floor and the ceiling.

For example, Python provides the built-in `round()` function and the `math.floor()` and `math.ceil()` functions for transforming floating point values to integers.

Rounding can lead to surprising results as the algorithm propagates the replacement of digits in a right-to-left order.

Therefore, it is generally preferred to use truncation of additional precision.

This is the direct deletion of the additional precision (e.g. in a report) or the presentation to a limited level of precision (e.g. in formatted output).

Regardless of the method chosen, once chosen, the same method must be used in all cases for consistency.

11.2.5   Tip 05: Avoid Scientific Notation

Scientific notation refers to a number representation that is more compact than a decimal number with full precision.

> Scientific notation is a way of expressing numbers that are too large or too small to be conveniently written in

> decimal form, since to do so would require writing out an inconveniently long string of digits.

– Scientific notation, Wikipedia.

A typical approach is to represent a decimal number with a base (b), an exponent (n), and a multiple (m).

For example: $m \times b^n$

The base could be e, a shorthand for "times ten raised to the power of some exponent". For example: $m \times en$

The exponent may be positive for large numbers or negative for very small numbers.

The measure adds the detail to the number, the specific details of the number.

Scientific notation is helpful when programming for brevity, but generally not helpful when presenting results.

This is because few people understand it well, at least at the time it needs to be understood in a report, and the conversion from the notation to a comparable number adds additional cognitive load.

Always use a decimal notation when presenting results.

11.3 Tips For Benchmark Measure Units

Units of measure refer to what the measure represents.

The default measure for almost all measurement functions is seconds, although nanosecond versions of most functions do exist.

Seconds may or may not be the best measure to use for a given set of benchmark results.

11.3.1   Tip 01: Know The Difference Between Units

Recall that units of time have names at each order of magnitude (times 10).

There are many, but we don't need to know them all.

Keep the following scale of measurements in mind:

Order	Name	Abbreviation
10^{-9}	nanosecond	ns
10^{-6}	microsecond	us
10^{-3}	millisecond	ms
10^{0}	second	s or sec

Note the jumps of 3 in the exponent, this is 3 zeros or 3 orders of magnitude, meaning we multiply or divide by 1,000 to go from one unit to the next.

For reference

- One second has 1,000 milliseconds.
- One millisecond has 1,000 microseconds.
- One microsecond has 1,000 nanoseconds.

Use one of these 4 measures if under a minute.

Above one minute, use the regular units of time, such as minutes and hours.

11.3.2   Tip 02: Don't Report A Score Too Low In Scale

Select a unit of measure that ensures the focus of the scores is close to the decimal point, e.g. just above or just below.

Choosing a measure that moves the focus to above the decimal point is probably the most helpful.

Choosing a unit of measure that is too low on the scale will mean that the differences of interest will be pushed far into the integers, such as thousands or millions.

This will look strange and add unnecessary cognitive load.

11.3.3 Tip 03: Don't Report A Score Too High In Scale

We can be too aggressive and choose a unit of measure that is too high on the scale.

Overcorrecting in this way may mean that the interesting parts of the measure are past the decimal point, perhaps requiring the addition of more precision in the results.

This will begin raising a conflict with the tips in the previous section of showing too much precision in results.

11.3.4 Tip 04: Default To Seconds If Unsure

Most Python functions for recording time operate at the level of seconds.

Everyone understands seconds and perhaps few people understand the difference between a nanosecond and a microsecond.

A good default is to stick with seconds and avoid conversions and new units of measure that require explanation.

This may mean choosing the code under study so that it is able to be completed in a reasonable number of seconds where difference can be captured in less than 3 orders of magnitude above and below the decimal point, e.g. `xxx.yyy seconds`.

11.3.5 Tip 05: Always Include The Units

When presenting a result, always include the units.

Use the full name or the common abbreviation.

For example:

```
Took 10.123 seconds
```

If it is a statistical quantity, like an average, clearly state this along with the units.

For example:

```
Took 10.123 seconds on average
```

11.4 Further Reading

This section lists helpful additional resources on the topic.

11.4.1 References

- Rounding, Wikipedia.
  https://en.wikipedia.org/wiki/Rounding
- Scientific notation, Wikipedia.
  https://en.wikipedia.org/wiki/Scientific_notation
- Unit of time, Wikipedia.
  https://en.wikipedia.org/wiki/Unit_of_time
- Orders of magnitude (time), Wikipedia.
  https://en.wikipedia.org/wiki/Orders_of_magnitude_(time)

11.4.2 APIs

- Python Built-in Functions.
  https://docs.python.org/3/library/functions.html

11.5 Takeaways

You now know helpful tips to consider when presenting execution time benchmark results.

Specifically, you know:

- Why collecting benchmark results is one step in a broader project.
- How to consider the precision when presenting benchmark results.
- How to consider the units of measure when presenting benchmark results.

11.5.1 Next

In the next tutorial, we will explore how to develop benchmark helper functions and classes.

Part IV

Benchmarking Helpers

We have seen how to record the execution time of statements, functions and whole programs.

It typically involves the same boilerplate code recording start time, end time, calculating the duration and reporting the measure.

We can hide this boilerplate behind helper code, such as:

- Helper functions.
- Helper objects.
- Helper context managers.
- Helper function decorators.

Hiding the benchmark code in this way means that we can easily benchmark ad hoc code with the addition of a function call or a function decorator.

It also ensures that the benchmarking procedure is consistent and bug free. We write it once, get it right, then reuse it again and again.

The following chapters explore how to develop a suite of different benchmarking helpers.

Chapter 12

Benchmark Helper Function

You can develop a helper function to benchmark target functions in Python.

This requires defining a custom helper class for executing a target function that automatically records and reports the overall execution time of the target function.

In this tutorial, you will discover how to develop and use a benchmark helper function to benchmark target functions in Python.

After completing this tutorial, you will know:

- How to use helper functions for benchmarking target functions.
- How to develop a helper function for one-off benchmarking.
- How to develop a helper function for repeated benchmarking.

Let's get started.

12.1 How To Develop A Benchmark Function

We can develop a helper function to automatically benchmark our Python code.

Let's explore two versions of a benchmark helper function:

1. One-off benchmark helper function.
2. Repeated benchmark helper function.

12.1.1   One-Off Benchmark Helper Function

Our helper function can take the name of our target function that we wish to benchmark as an argument along with any arguments to the target function.

For example:

```
# benchmark function
def benchmark(fun, *args):
    # ...
```

The `*args` argument is an optional list of function arguments to the target function.

It allows us to specify zero, one, or many arguments for our target function to the benchmark function, which we can pass on to the target function directly, for example:

```
...
# call the custom function
fun(*args)
```

Our function can then record the start time, call the target function, record the end time, and report the overall execution time.

We will use the `time.perf_counter()` time function, preferred for benchmarking.

For example:

```
...
# record start time
time_start = perf_counter()
# call the custom function
fun(*args)
# record end time
```

```
time_end = perf_counter()
# calculate the duration
time_duration = time_end - time_start
# report the duration
print(f'Took {time_duration:.3f} seconds')
```

Tying this together a helper function for benchmarking arbitrary Python functions is listed below.

```
# benchmark function
def benchmark(fun, *args):
    # record start time
    time_start = perf_counter()
    # call the custom function
    fun(*args)
    # record end time
    time_end = perf_counter()
    # calculate the duration
    time_duration = time_end - time_start
    # report the duration
    print(f'Took {time_duration:.3f} seconds')
```

It requires that we import the `time.perf_counter` function, but this could be imported into the function directly if we choose.

For example:

```
# benchmark function
def benchmark(fun, *args):
    # import required function
    from time import perf_counter
    ...
```

12.1.2 Repeated Benchmark Helper Function

It is good practice to repeat a benchmark task a few times and report the average execution time.

We can repeat the benchmark by updating our function to take a number of repeats as an argument.

For example:

```
# repeated benchmark function
def repeated_benchmark(fun, n_repeats, *args):
    # ...
```

We can then loop the main benchmark operation and store the results of each iteration in a list.

```
...
results = list()
# repeat the benchmark many times
for i in range(n_repeats):
    # record start time
    time_start = perf_counter()
    # call the custom function
    fun(*args)
    # record end time
    time_end = perf_counter()
    # calculate the duration
    time_duration = time_end - time_start
    # store the result
    results.append(time_duration)
    # report progress
    print(f'>{i+1} took {time_duration:.3f} sec')
```

Finally, at the end of the repeats, we can calculate the average duration and report the final result.

```
...
# calculate average duration
avg_duration = sum(results) / n_repeats
# report the average duration
print(f'Took {avg_duration:.3f} sec on average')
```

Tying this together, the complete example of a repeated benchmark helper function is listed below.

```python
# repeated benchmark function
def repeated_benchmark(fun, n_repeats, *args):
    results = list()
    # repeat the benchmark many times
    for i in range(n_repeats):
        # record start time
        time_start = perf_counter()
        # call the custom function
        fun(*args)
        # record end time
        time_end = perf_counter()
        # calculate the duration
        time_duration = time_end - time_start
        # store the result
        results.append(time_duration)
        # report progress
        print(f'>{i+1} took {time_duration:.3f} sec')
    # calculate average duration
    avg_duration = sum(results) / n_repeats
    # report the average duration
    print(f'Took {avg_duration:.3f} sec on average')
```

Now that we know how to develop benchmark helper functions, let's explore some worked examples.

12.2 Example of Benchmarking Using Helper Function

We can explore how to use our one-off benchmark helper function to benchmark the execution time of a custom function.

In this example, we will define a custom function that takes a moment to complete.

The function creates a list of 100 million squared integers in a list comprehension.

For example:

```
# function to benchmark
def task():
    # create a large list
    data = [i*i for i in range(100000000)]
```

We can then call our **benchmark()** function and pass it the name of our target function, in this case, **task**.

. . .

```
# benchmark the task() function
benchmark(task)
```

And that's it.

Tying this together, the complete example of using our helper benchmark function to estimate the duration of our **task()** target function is listed below.

```
# SuperFastPython.com
# example of benchmarking using a custom function
from time import perf_counter

# benchmark function
def benchmark(fun, *args):
    # record start time
    time_start = perf_counter()
    # call the custom function
    fun(*args)
    # record end time
    time_end = perf_counter()
    # calculate the duration
    time_duration = time_end - time_start
    # report the duration
    print(f'Took {time_duration:.3f} seconds')

# function to benchmark
def task():
    # create a large list
```

```
    data = [i*i for i in range(100000000)]

# protect the entry point
if __name__ == '__main__':
    # benchmark the task() function
    benchmark(task)
```

Running the program calls the `benchmark()` function.

The benchmark function runs and records the start time.

It then calls the target function with any arguments provided to the helper function, in this case, no arguments.

The task function runs normally and returns.

The benchmark function records the end time and then calculates the execution time duration.

The duration is then reported.

In this case, we can see that the `task()` function took about 6.275 seconds to complete.

Note, the results on your system may differ.

This highlights how we can benchmark arbitrary functions using our benchmark helper function.

```
Took 6.275 seconds
```

Next, let's explore an example of using our repeated benchmark function.

12.3 Example Of Repeated Benchmarking With Helper

We can explore how to repeatedly benchmark our target function.

In this example, we will use our `repeated_benchmark()` helper function with three repeats to estimate the average run time of our `task()` function.

This requires calling our **repeated_benchmark()** function and specifying the name of the target function, the number of repeats (e.g. 3),
and any arguments to the task function (there are none).

For example:

```
...
# benchmark the task() function
repeated_benchmark(task, 3)
```

Tying this together, the complete example is listed below.

```
# SuperFastPython.com
# example of benchmarking using a custom function
from time import perf_counter

# repeated benchmark function
def repeated_benchmark(fun, n_repeats, *args):
    results = list()
    # repeat the benchmark many times
    for i in range(n_repeats):
        # record start time
        time_start = perf_counter()
        # call the custom function
        fun(*args)
        # record end time
        time_end = perf_counter()
        # calculate the duration
        time_duration = time_end - time_start
        # store the result
        results.append(time_duration)
        # report progress
        print(f'>{i+1} took {time_duration:.3f} sec')
    # calculate average duration
    avg_duration = sum(results) / n_repeats
    # report the average duration
    print(f'Took {avg_duration:.3f} sec on average')
```

```
# function to benchmark
def task():
    # create a large list
    data = [i*i for i in range(100000000)]

# protect the entry point
if __name__ == '__main__':
    # benchmark the task() function
    repeated_benchmark(task, 3)
```

Running the program calls the `repeated_benchmark()` function.

The benchmark function runs the main benchmark loop.

Each iteration, the loop records the start time. It then calls the target function with any arguments provided to the helper function, in this case, no arguments. The task function runs normally and returns. The benchmark function records the end time and then calculates the duration and reports it as a progress indicator.

This is repeated three times.

Finally, the average of all runs is calculated and then reported.

In this case, we can see that the `task()` function took about 6.146 seconds to complete on average.

Note, the results on your system may differ.

This highlights how we can repeatedly benchmark arbitrary functions using our benchmark helper function.

```
>1 took 6.260 sec
>2 took 6.171 sec
>3 took 6.005 sec
Took 6.146 sec on average
```

12.4   Further Reading

This section lists helpful additional resources on the topic.

- `time` – Time access and conversions.
  https://docs.python.org/3/library/time.html

12.5   Takeaways

You now know how to develop and use a benchmark helper function to benchmark functions in Python.

Specifically, you know:

- How to use helper functions for benchmarking target functions.
- How to develop a helper function for one-off benchmarking.
- How to develop a helper function for repeated benchmarking.

12.5.1   Next

In the next tutorial, we will explore how to develop a stopwatch class.

Chapter 13

Benchmark Stopwatch Class

You can develop a stopwatch timer class to benchmark the execution time of code.

This requires defining a custom class that provides methods for starting and stopping the timer and using the timer instance within code that is to be benchmarked.

In this tutorial, you will discover how to develop a stopwatch timer class for benchmarking in Python.

After completing this tutorial, you will know:

- How to develop a stopwatch class for arbitrary benchmarking.
- How to develop a stopwatch class that can be paused and resumed.
- How to use a custom stopwatch class to benchmark code.

Let's get started.

13.1 How To Develop A Stopwatch Timer Class

We can develop a stopwatch timer class.

Generally, the class provides a method to start the timer, a method to stop the timer, and a method to get the duration that the timer was running.

We will explore two versions of the timer:

1. Simple single-use timer.
2. Timer that can be resumed.

Let's dive in.

13.1.1   Simple Stopwatch Timer

We can develop a simple stopwatch timer.

The timer provides three methods:

1. `start()`: starts the timer, and records the current time.
2. `stop()`: stops the timer, and records the current time.
3. `duration()`: returns the difference between end and start times

And that's it.

We will use the `time.perf_counter()` time function to record the time, which preferred for benchmarking.

Tying this together, the `StopwatchTimer` class below implements this.

```python
# custom stopwatch timer class
class StopwatchTimer:
    # start the timer
    def start(self):
        self.time_start = perf_counter()
    # stop the timer
    def stop(self):
        self.time_end = perf_counter()
    # get the duration
    def duration(self):
        return self.time_end - self.time_start
```

We could change the design slightly to calculate and record the duration when the **stop()** method is called and then simply return it in the duration method.

I prefer tracking the start and stop times and making them available if needed and computing the duration derived from those recorded details.

To start the timer we create an instance and call the **start()** method:

```
...
# create the timer
timer = StopwatchTimer()
# start the timer
timer.start()
```

To stop the timer, we call the **stop()** method:

```
...
# stop the timer
timer.stop()
```

Then, if we want to report the duration, we can call the **duration()** method and print the result:

```
...
# report the duration
print(timer.duration())
```

The timer could be reused by calling **start()** and **stop()** again in the same order. This will overwrite the internal state attributes correctly.

This timer cannot be resumed again if stopped.

Next, let's look at how we might update the **StopwatchTimer** class to add the ability to resume the timer after it has been stopped.

13.1.2   Stopwatch Timer With Resume Support

We can update the stopwatch timer class developed in the previous section to add resume support.

Resume support can be added by updating the `stop()` method to calculate the duration since `start()` was called and adding the result to an internal attribute.

For example:

```
# stop the timer
def stop(self):
    time_end = perf_counter()
    self.sum_duration += time_end - self.time_start
```

This allows each combination of `start()` and `stop()` to be accumulated and returned via the call to `duration()`.

We can then add a new method to reset the internal duration accumulation, which must be called in order to reuse the timer.

```
# reset the timer
def reset(self):
    self.sum_duration = 0
```

It is also a good idea to reset the timer the first time in the constructor.

```
# constructor
def __init__(self):
    self.reset()
```

And that's it, tying this together, the `ResumeStopwatchTimer` class provides a reusable stopwatch timer for benchmarking.

```
# custom stopwatch timer class that can be resumed
class ResumeStopwatchTimer:
    # constructor
    def __init__(self):
        self.reset()
    # start or resume the timer
    def start(self):
        self.time_start = perf_counter()
    # stop the timer
    def stop(self):
```

```
        time_end = perf_counter()
        self.sum_duration += time_end - self.time_start
    # get the duration
    def duration(self):
        return self.sum_duration
    # reset the timer
    def reset(self):
        self.sum_duration = 0
```

We can then create the timer and call the **start()** method to start the timer.

```
...
# create the timer
timer = ResumeStopwatchTimer()
# start the timer
timer.start()
```

The timer can then be stopped and started again, then stopped.

```
...
# stop the timer
timer.stop()
# ...
# start the timer
timer.start()
...
# stop the timer
timer.stop()
```

Finally, we can retrieve and report the overall duration of all start-stop pairs and reset the timer for reuse.

```
...
# report the duration
print(timer.duration())
# reset the timer
timer.reset()
```

Now that we know how to develop a stopwatch timer, let's look at some worked examples.

13.2 Example Of Using A Stopwatch Timer

We can explore an example of benchmarking code using the simple `StopwatchTimer` class.

In this case, we will create a list of 100 million squared integers, which should take a few seconds.

This requires first creating the stopwatch and starting the timer.

```
...
# create the timer
timer = StopwatchTimer()
# start the timer
timer.start()
```

We can then run our target code.

```
...
# create a list of squared numbers
result = [i*i for i in range(100000000)]
```

Finally, we can stop the timer and report the duration in seconds.

```
...
# stop the timer
timer.stop()
# report the duration
print(f'Took {timer.duration()} seconds')
```

Tying this together, the complete example is listed below.

```
# SuperFastPython.com
# example of a custom stopwatch timer class
from time import perf_counter

# custom stopwatch timer class
class StopwatchTimer:
```

```
    # start the timer
    def start(self):
        self.time_start = perf_counter()
    # stop the timer
    def stop(self):
        self.time_end = perf_counter()
    # get the duration
    def duration(self):
        return self.time_end - self.time_start

# create the timer
timer = StopwatchTimer()
# start the timer
timer.start()
# create a list of squared numbers
result = [i*i for i in range(100000000)]
# stop the timer
timer.stop()
# report the duration
print(f'Took {timer.duration()} seconds')
```

Running the example first creates and starts the timer.

The list of squared integers is then created, which takes a moment.

Finally, the timer is stopped and the result is reported.

In this case, we can see that the task took about 5.103 seconds.

Note, the results on your system may differ.

This highlights how we can use the simple benchmark timer class.

```
Took 5.1031060218811035 seconds
```

Next, let's explore how we might use the stopwatch timer class that can be resumed.

13.3 Example Of Using A Stopwatch Timer With Resume

We can explore an example of using the stopwatch timer that can be resumed.

In this case, we will first time one target statement, stop the timer, then resume the timer to time a second statement. Finally, we will report the combined duration of both statements.

This involves first creating and starting the `ResumeStopwatchTimer`, executing the first statement, then stopping the timer and reporting the duration.

```
...
# create the timer
timer = ResumeStopwatchTimer()
# start the timer
timer.start()
# create a list of squared numbers
result = [i*i for i in range(100000000)]
# stop the timer
timer.stop()
# report the duration
print(f'Took {timer.duration()} seconds')
```

We can then resume the timer by calling the **start()** method, executing the second statement, stopping the timer, and reporting the overall duration of both statements.

```
...
# resume the timer
timer.start()
# do some more work
result = [i*i for i in range(100000000)]
# stop the timer
timer.stop()
# report the duration
print(f'Took {timer.duration()} seconds')
```

Tying this together, the complete example is listed below.

```python
# SuperFastPython.com
# example of a custom stopwatch timer class with resume
from time import perf_counter

# custom stopwatch timer class that can be resumed
class ResumeStopwatchTimer:
    # constructor
    def __init__(self):
        self.reset()
    # start or resume the timer
    def start(self):
        self.time_start = perf_counter()
    # stop the timer
    def stop(self):
        time_end = perf_counter()
        self.sum_duration += time_end - self.time_start
    # get the duration
    def duration(self):
        return self.sum_duration
    # reset the timer
    def reset(self):
        self.sum_duration = 0

# create the timer
timer = ResumeStopwatchTimer()
# start the timer
timer.start()
# create a list of squared numbers
result = [i*i for i in range(100000000)]
# stop the timer
timer.stop()
# report the duration
print(f'Took {timer.duration()} seconds')
# resume the timer
timer.start()
```

```
# do some more work
result = [i*i for i in range(100000000)]
# stop the timer
timer.stop()
# report the duration
print(f'Took {timer.duration()} seconds')
```

Running the example first creates and starts the timer.

Next, the target code is executed, the timer is stopped and the duration is reported.

In this case, the target code takes about 5.012 seconds to complete.

The timer is then resumed, and the second target statement is executed. The timer is stopped again and the overall duration of the timer is reported.

In this case, the summed duration of the two statements is reported as about 10.841 seconds.

Note, the results on your system may differ.

This highlights how we can stop and resume a timer to calculate the overall duration of multiple sections of code.

```
Took 5.012497186660767 seconds
Took 10.84142518043518 seconds
```

13.4   Further Reading

This section lists helpful additional resources on the topic.

- **time** – Time access and conversions.
  https://docs.python.org/3/library/time.html

13.5   Takeaways

You now know how to develop a stopwatch timer class for benchmarking in Python.

Specifically, you know:

- How to develop a stopwatch class for arbitrary benchmarking.
- How to develop a stopwatch class that can be paused and resumed.
- How to use a custom stopwatch class to benchmark code.

13.5.1   Next

In the next tutorial, we will explore how to develop a benchmark context manager.

Chapter 14

Benchmark Context Manager

You can develop a custom context manager to automatically benchmark code in Python.

This requires defining a custom context manager class and then embedding target code to be benchmarked within the context manager body block.

In this tutorial, you will discover how to benchmark Python code using a context manager.

After completing this tutorial, you will know:

- How to develop a context manager for benchmarking.
- How to use a custom context manager for benchmarking blocks of code.

Let's get started.

14.1 How To Benchmark Code Using A Context Manager

We can develop our custom context manager to automatically benchmark blocks of code

Firstly, let's review context managers.

14.1.1 Context Managers

A context manager is used via the `with` expression and provides context for a block of code executed within.

> A context manager is an object that defines the runtime context to be established when executing a with statement. The context manager handles the entry into, and the exit from, the desired runtime context for the execution of the block of code.

– Python Data model.

A context manager is implemented as a Python object that has `__enter__()` and `__exit__()` methods and is used via the `with` expression.

The `__enter__()` method defines what happens at the beginning of a block, such as opening or preparing resources, like a file, socket or thread pool.

The `__exit__()` method defines what happens when the block is exited, such as closing a prepared resource.

An example include opening a file via the `open()` built-in function.

For example:

```
...
# open a file and read content
with open('/path/to/file.txt', 'r') as file:
    data = file.read()
```

And that's about all we need to know about context managers, for now.

Next, let's look at how we can define custom context managers to automatically benchmark blocks of code.

14.1.2   Benchmark Context Manager

We can define a new class that implements a constructor `__init__()` and the `__enter__()` and `__exit__()` methods.

The `__init__()` constructor can take a name argument for the benchmark case and store it in an object attribute. This is strictly not required but is helpful in the case where we reuse the same context manager many times in our program.

For example:

```
# constructor
def __init__(self, name):
    # store the name of this benchmark
    self.name = name
```

The `__enter__()` method can initialize the start time and store it in object attribute for use later.

We will use the `time.perf_counter()` time function, preferred for benchmarking.

For example:

```
...
# enter the context manager
def __enter__(self):
    # record the start time
    self.time_start = perf_counter()
    # return this object
    return self
```

The `__exit__()` method must take some standard arguments defined by the context manager interface.

The method will then record the end time, calculate and store the duration and report the calculated duration along with the name of the benchmark case.

```
...
# exit the context manager
def __exit__(self, exc_type, exc_value, traceback):
    # record the end time
    self.time_end = perf_counter()
    # calculate the duration
    self.duration = self.time_end - self.time_start
    # report the duration
    print(f'{self.name} took {self.duration:.3f} s')
    # do not suppress any exception
    return False
```

Tying this together, we can define our **Benchmark** context manager class below.

```
# define the benchmark context manager
class Benchmark:
    # constructor
    def __init__(self, name):
        # store the name of this benchmark
        self.name = name

    # enter the context manager
    def __enter__(self):
        # record the start time
        self.time_start = perf_counter()
        # return this object
        return self

    # exit the context manager
    def __exit__(self, exc_type, exc_value, traceback):
        # record the end time
        self.time_end = perf_counter()
        # calculate the duration
        self.duration = self.time_end - self.time_start
```

```
        # report the duration
        print(f'{self.name} took {self.duration:.3f} s')
        # do not suppress any exception
        return False
```

We can then use it by creating an instance of the **Benchmark** class within the **with** expression and then list any code within the context we wish to benchmark.

For example:

```
...
# create the benchmark context
with Benchmark('Task'):
    # run some code
    ...
```

The code within the context will run as per normal, and once finished, the total execution time will be reported automatically.

When benchmarking, we often prefer to repeat a benchmark many times and report a summary statistic, like the average. This is challenging to do with a custom benchmark context manager as we don't have direct control over re-executing the body or code block within the context manager. As such, we will not develop a version of a benchmark context manager capable of repeating a benchmark.

Now that we know how to develop and use a benchmark context manager, let's look at some examples.

14.2 Example Of Benchmarking With Context Manager

We can explore how to use our Benchmark context manager to benchmark the execution time of a custom function.

In this example, we will define a custom function that takes a moment to complete.

The function creates a list of 100 million squared integers in a list comprehension.

For example:

```
# function to benchmark
def task():
    # create a large list
    data = [i*i for i in range(100000000)]
```

We can then call this function within the Benchmark context manager to have the execution time automatically recorded and reported.

For example:

```
# create the benchmark context
with Benchmark('Task'):
    # run the task
    task()
```

Tying this together, the complete example is listed below.

```
# SuperFastPython.com
# example of a benchmark context manager
from time import perf_counter

# define the benchmark context manager
class Benchmark:
    # constructor
    def __init__(self, name):
        # store the name of this benchmark
        self.name = name

    # enter the context manager
    def __enter__(self):
        # record the start time
        self.time_start = perf_counter()
        # return this object
        return self
```

```
    # exit the context manager
    def __exit__(self, exc_type, exc_value, traceback):
        # record the end time
        self.time_end = perf_counter()
        # calculate the duration
        self.duration = self.time_end - self.time_start
        # report the duration
        print(f'{self.name} took {self.duration:.3f} s')
        # do not suppress any exception
        return False

# function to benchmark
def task():
    # create a large list
    data = [i*i for i in range(100000000)]

# protect the entry point
if __name__ == '__main__':
    # create the benchmark context
    with Benchmark('Task'):
        # run the task
        task()
```

Running the example first creates the Benchmark context manager within the with expression and provides the name **"Task"**, which is stored in an object attribute.

The context manager is entered, automatically calling the __enter__() method where the start time is recorded in an object attribute.

The task() function is then called and the list is created.

Finally, the context manager is exited, automatically calling the __exit__() method, recording the end time, calculating the duration, and reporting it to standard out.

In this case, we can see that the task() function took about 6.091 seconds to complete.

Note, the results on your system may differ.

This highlights how we can benchmark arbitrary code using a custom context manager.

```
Task took 6.091 s
```

14.3 Further Reading

This section lists helpful additional resources on the topic.

- `time` – Time access and conversions.
  https://docs.python.org/3/library/time.html
- Python Built-in Types.
  https://docs.python.org/3/library/stdtypes.html
- Python Data model.
  https://docs.python.org/3/reference/datamodel.html
- A Context Manager for Timing Benchmarks, Dave Beazley, 2010.
  http://dabeaz.blogspot.com/2010/02/context-manager-for-timing-benchmarks.html

14.4 Takeaways

You now know how to benchmark Python code using a context manager.

Specifically, you know:

- How to develop a context manager for benchmarking.
- How to use a custom context manager for benchmarking blocks of code.

14.4.1 Next

In the next tutorial, we will explore how to develop a benchmark function decorator.

Chapter 15

Benchmark Function Decorator

You can develop a custom benchmark decorator that will automatically record and report the execution time of target functions.

This requires defining the decorator function and adding the decoration to the function to be benchmarked.

In this tutorial, you will discover how to automatically benchmark target functions using a benchmark decorator in Python.

After completing this tutorial, you will know:

- How to develop a function decorator to automatically benchmark a target function.
- How to develop a function decorator for repeated benchmarking of a target function.
- How to use a custom function decorator to benchmark a target function.

Let's get started.

15.1 How To Develop A Benchmark Function Decorator

We can develop our custom function decorator to automatically benchmark our target functions.

Firstly, let's review function decorators.

15.1.1 Function Decorators

A function decorator in Python allows a custom function to be called automatically that will in turn call our target function.

This can be used to insert code before and after calling our target function, such as recording the start time, and end time, and calculating an overall execution duration.

A function decorator can be defined as a custom function that returns a function that in turn calls our target function.

Typically, the new separate function is defined as an inner function, that is, within the called function.

For example:

```
# define the custom decorator
def custom_decorator(func):
    # inner function that wraps the target function
    def inner_wrapper():
        # call the target function
        func()
```

The decorator can be added to arbitrary functions in our program as follows:

```
# function that has the decorator
@custom_decorator
def task():
    # ...
```

The function we are adding the decorator to, e.g. `task()` may take arguments and may have a return value.

Therefore our inner wrapper function needs to handle this accordingly.

For example:

```
# define the custom decorator
def custom_decorator(func):
    # inner function that wraps the target function
    def inner_wrapper(*args, **kwargs):
        # call the target function
        return func(*args, **kwargs)
```

Additionally, we may want to leave the decorator on the target function and have the function look and feel unchanged, e.g. if we print the function or call `help()` on the function. With the decorator in place, this will not be the case.

Instead, we can have the decorator look like the target function passed in, so that any interrogation of the target function looks normal.

This can be achieved by adding the `functools.wraps` decorator to our inner wrapper function.

> This is a convenience function for invoking `update_wrapper()` as a function decorator when defining a wrapper function. [...] Without the use of this decorator factory, the name of the example function would have been 'wrapper', and the docstring of the original `example()` would have been lost.

– `functools` – Higher-order functions and operations on callable objects.

For example:

```
# define the custom decorator
def custom_decorator(func):
    # inner function that wraps the target function
    @wraps(func)
```

```
def inner_wrapper(*args, **kwargs):
    # call the target function
    return func(*args, **kwargs)
```

And that's about it for decorators for now.

Next, let's look at how we can define custom decorators to automatically benchmark our target functions.

15.1.2   One-Off Benchmark Function Decorator

We can develop a function decorator to benchmark a function automatically.

The decorator will be called **benchmark_decorator()** and takes the function name to be decorated as an argument.

```
# define the benchmark decorator
def benchmark_decorator(func):
    # ...
```

Next, we can define the inner wrapper function.

It must take arguments for the target function, just in case. It then must record the start time before calling the function, and the end time after calling the function.

We will use the **time.perf_counter()** time function, preferred for benchmarking.

It then calculates the duration and reports it before returning any return value from the target function itself.

For example:

```
# inner function that wraps the target function
@wraps(func)
def wrapper(*args, **kwargs):
    # record start time
    time_start = perf_counter()
    # call the custom function
```

```
    result = func(*args, **kwargs)
    # record end time
    time_end = perf_counter()
    # calculate the duration
    time_duration = time_end - time_start
    # report the duration
    print(f'Took {time_duration:.3f} s')
    # pass on the return value
    return result
```

Tying this together, the complete function decorator for benchmarking target functions is listed below.

```
# define the benchmark decorator
def benchmark_decorator(func):
    # inner function that wraps the target function
    @wraps(func)
    def wrapper(*args, **kwargs):
        # record start time
        time_start = perf_counter()
        # call the custom function
        result = func(*args, **kwargs)
        # record end time
        time_end = perf_counter()
        # calculate the duration
        time_duration = time_end - time_start
        # report the duration
        print(f'Took {time_duration:.3f} s')
        # pass on the return value
        return result
    # return the inner function
    return wrapper
```

Finally, to use the decorator, we add `@benchmark_decorator` to the definition of the target function.

For example:

```
@benchmark_decorator
def custom_function():
    # ...
```

Next, let's look at how we might update the decorator to report the average execution time.

15.1.3   Repeated Benchmark Function Decorator

It can be a good idea to repeat a benchmark many times and report the average execution time.

This is because each benchmark score may be slightly different due to the Python interpreter having to load modules for the first time, the Python garbage collector, and other programs running in the background of the system at the same time.

We can update the benchmark function decorator from the last section to calculate the average execution time instead of a one-off execution time.

This will require executing the target function multiple times, e.g. 3, which could have side effects if the function is changing the program state.

We can update the internal **wrapper()** function to loop three times, and each iteration benchmarks the target function.

The scores can be collected in a list.

```
...
results = list()
# repeat the benchmark many times
n_repeats = 3
for i in range(n_repeats):
    # record start time
    time_start = perf_counter()
    # call the custom function
    result = func(*args, **kwargs)
    # record end time
```

```
time_end = perf_counter()
# calculate the duration
time_duration = time_end - time_start
# store the result
results.append(time_duration)
# report progress
print(f'>{i+1} took {time_duration:.3f} s')
```

After all executions of the target function, we can calculate the average execution time and report the result, before returning the final return value from the target function.

```
...
# calculate average duration
avg_duration = sum(results) / n_repeats
# report the average duration
print(f'Took {avg_duration:.3f} sec on average')
# pass on the return value
return result
```

Tying this together, the complete updated benchmark decorator is listed below.

```
# define the average benchmark decorator
def average_benchmark_decorator(func):
    # inner function that wraps the target function
    @wraps(func)
    def wrapper(*args, **kwargs):
        results = list()
        # repeat the benchmark many times
        n_repeats = 3
        for i in range(n_repeats):
            # record start time
            time_start = perf_counter()
            # call the custom function
            result = func(*args, **kwargs)
            # record end time
            time_end = perf_counter()
```

```
        # calculate the duration
        time_duration = time_end - time_start
        # store the result
        results.append(time_duration)
        # report progress
        print(f'>{i+1} took {time_duration:.3f} s')
    # calculate average duration
    avg_duration = sum(results) / n_repeats
    # report the average duration
    print(f'Took {avg_duration:.3f} sec on average')
    # pass on the return value
    return result
  # return the inner function
  return wrapper
```

As above, this would be used by adding the decorator to the definition of the target function.

For example:

```
@average_benchmark_decorator
def custom_function():
    # ...
```

Now that we know how to develop a benchmark function decorator, let's look at some worked examples.

15.2   Example Of Benchmarking With Function Decorator

We can explore how to use our one-off benchmark function decorator to benchmark the execution time of a custom function.

In this example, we will define a custom function that takes a moment to complete.

The function creates a list of 100 million squared integers in a list comprehension.

For example:

```
# function to benchmark
def task():
    # create a large list
    data = [i*i for i in range(100000000)]
```

We can then add our `@benchmark_decorator` decoration to our `task()` function.

```
# function to benchmark, with benchmark decorator
@benchmark_decorator
def task():
    # create a large list
    data = [i*i for i in range(100000000)]
```

Then, all we need to do is call the `task()` function from the entry point of the program and it will be benchmarked automatically.

Tying this together, the complete example of using our function decorator to estimate the duration of our `task()` target function is listed below.

```
# SuperFastPython.com
# example of benchmarking using a decorator
from time import perf_counter
from functools import wraps

# define the benchmark decorator
def benchmark_decorator(func):
    # inner function that wraps the target function
    @wraps(func)
    def wrapper(*args, **kwargs):
        # record start time
        time_start = perf_counter()
        # call the custom function
        result = func(*args, **kwargs)
        # record end time
        time_end = perf_counter()
```

```
        # calculate the duration
        time_duration = time_end - time_start
        # report the duration
        print(f'Took {time_duration:.3f} seconds')
        # pass on the return value
        return result
    # return the inner function
    return wrapper

# function to benchmark, with benchmark decorator
@benchmark_decorator
def task():
    # create a large list
    data = [i*i for i in range(100000000)]

# protect the entry point
if __name__ == '__main__':
    # call the custom function
    task()
```

Running the program calls the `task()` function.

The benchmark decorator runs and records the start time.

It then calls the target `task()` function with any arguments provided to the helper function, in this case, no arguments, and retrieves the return value.

The task function runs normally and returns.

The benchmark function records the end time and then calculates the duration.

The duration is then reported to the standard output.

In this case, we can see that the `task()` function took about 6.441 seconds to complete.

Note, the results on your system may differ.

This highlights how we can benchmark arbitrary functions using our benchmark function decorator.

```
Took 6.441 seconds
```

Next, let's look at how we might report the average execution time using our repeated benchmark decorator.

15.3 Example Of Repeated Benchmarking

We can explore how to repeatedly benchmark our target function using a decorator.

In this example, we will use our `benchmark_decorator()` decorator developed above which has three repeated benchmark runs to estimate the average run time of our `task()` function.

We can then change the decorator above our target function.

```
# function to benchmark, with benchmark decorator
@average_benchmark_decorator
def task():
    # create a large list
    data = [i*i for i in range(100000000)]
```

And that's it.

Tying this together, the complete example is listed below.

```
# SuperFastPython.com
# example of benchmarking average time using a decorator
from time import perf_counter
from functools import wraps

# define the average benchmark decorator
def average_benchmark_decorator(func):
    # inner function that wraps the target function
    @wraps(func)
    def wrapper(*args, **kwargs):
```

```
        results = list()
        # repeat the benchmark many times
        n_repeats = 3
        for i in range(n_repeats):
            # record start time
            time_start = perf_counter()
            # call the custom function
            result = func(*args, **kwargs)
            # record end time
            time_end = perf_counter()
            # calculate the duration
            time_duration = time_end - time_start
            # store the result
            results.append(time_duration)
            # report progress
            print(f'>{i+1} took {time_duration:.3f} s')
        # calculate average duration
        avg_duration = sum(results) / n_repeats
        # report the average duration
        print(f'Took {avg_duration:.3f} sec on average')
        # pass on the return value
        return result
    # return the inner function
    return wrapper

# function to benchmark, with benchmark decorator
@average_benchmark_decorator
def task():
    # create a large list
    data = [i*i for i in range(100000000)]

# protect the entry point
if __name__ == '__main__':
    # call the custom function
    task()
```

Running the program calls our custom `task()` function.

The benchmark decorator runs the main benchmark loop.

Each iteration, the loop records the start time. It then calls the target function with any arguments provided to the helper function, in this case, no arguments.

The task function runs normally and returns. The benchmark decorator records the end time and then calculates the duration and reports it as a progress indicator.

This is repeated three times.

Finally, the average of all runs is calculated and then reported.

In this case, we can see that the `task()` function took about 6.136 seconds to complete on average.

Note, the results on your system may differ.

This highlights how we can automatically calculate and report the average execution time for a target function using a custom benchmark decorator.

```
>1 took 6.191 s
>2 took 6.077 s
>3 took 6.138 s
Took 6.136 sec on average
```

15.4   Further Reading

This section lists helpful additional resources on the topic.

- `time` – Time access and conversions.
  https://docs.python.org/3/library/time.html
- `functools` – Higher-order functions and operations on callable objects.
  https://docs.python.org/3/library/functools.html

15.5   Takeaways

You now know how to automatically benchmark target functions using a benchmark decorator in Python.

Specifically, you know:

- How to develop a function decorator to automatically benchmark a target function.
- How to develop a function decorator for repeated benchmarking of a target function.
- How to use a custom function decorator to benchmark a target function.

15.5.1   Next

In the next tutorial, we will explore how to benchmark asyncio programs.

Part V

Benchmarking Asyncio

Asyncio programs are different to regular Python programs.

Asyncio refers to the changes to the Python language to support coroutines and the `asyncio` module that provides the event loop and tools for running asynchronous programs.

The asyncio event loop maintains its own timer, and we can use this to measure the execution time in our asyncio programs.

Additionally, the helper functions and classes we developed in prior chapters won't work in asyncio programs, as they may result in a syntax error.

Therefore, we have to develop asyncio-specific versions of helpers, such as: helper coroutines and asynchronous context managers.

The following chapters explore how we can benchmark asyncio programs, starting with a gentle introduction to asynchronous programming in Python.

Chapter 16

Gentle Introduction to Asyncio

You can implement asynchronous programming in Python using asyncio.

Asynchronous programming is a programming paradigm that allows you to write code that can perform multiple tasks concurrently without waiting for each task to complete before starting the next one.

It enables more efficient use of system resources and can significantly improve the responsiveness and performance of applications, particularly in scenarios where there are long-running operations, such as I/O operations or network requests.

In this tutorial we will take a whirlwind tour of Python concurrency.

After completing this tutorial, you will know:

- What is asyncio and how does it relate to threading and multiprocessing.
- How to use the async and await syntax.
- How to define, create, and run custom coroutines in an asyncio program.

Let's get started.

16.1 Python Concurrency Overview

Concurrency refers to parts of a program that are independent and can be executed out of order.

For example, a part in our program may comprise multiple tasks that do not need to interact with each other and can be completed in any order as long as they are all completed, such as loading multiple separate files.

Concurrent tasks may or may not be executed in parallel. Parallelism refers explicitly to the ability to execute tasks simultaneously, such as with multiple CPU cores.

The Python standard library provides four main modules for concurrency, they are:

- `multiprocessing`: for process-based concurrency with the `multiprocessing.Process` class.
- `threading`: for thread-based concurrency with the `threading.Thread` class.
- `concurrent.futures`: for thread and process pools that use the executor design pattern.
- `asyncio`: for coroutine-based concurrency for non-blocking I/O.

Only Processes provide true parallelism in Python, that is the ability to execute tasks simultaneously on multiple CPUs. This is achieved by starting new child instances of the Python interpreter process for executing tasks. Data sharing between processes is achieved via inter-process communication in which data must be serialized at added computational cost.

Python Threads provide concurrency, but only limited parallelism. This is because of the Global Interpreter Lock (GIL) that ensures the Python interpreter is thread safe by limiting only a single thread to execute at any one time within a Python process. The GIL is released in some situations, such as performing I/O operations, allowing modest parallel execution when interacting with files, sockets, and devices.

Asynchronous I/O, or Asyncio for short, is an implementation of asynchronous programming that provides the ability to create and run coroutines within an event-loop. A coroutine is a type of routine that can be suspended and resumed, allowing the asyncio event loop to jump from one to another when instructed. The paradigm provides a limited set of non-blocking I/O operations.

Each of processes, threads, and asyncio has a sweet spot.

- Processes are suited for CPU-bound tasks, but are limited to perhaps tens of tasks and have overhead in sharing data between processes.
- Threads are suited to I/O-bound tasks, but are limited to perhaps thousands of tasks.
- Asyncio is suited to large-scale I/O-bound tasks, e.g. perhaps tens of thousands of tasks, but are limited to a subset of non-blocking I/O operations and require adopting the asynchronous programming paradigm.

Now that we have a high-level understanding of the concurrency capabilities provided by the Python standard library, let's take a closer look at asyncio.

16.2 How To Use Asyncio

Python provides an **asyncio** module for Asynchronous Programming and specifically Asynchronous Input/Output.

It primarily provides a way to create and run coroutines using the async/await syntax.

A coroutine is a programming pattern that generalizes routines (e.g. subroutines, functions, or blocks of code) to allow them to be suspended and resumed.

Coroutines use cooperative multitasking, requiring the thread of execution to explicitly yield control by awaiting.

A coroutine can be defined via the `async def` expression; for example:

```
# define a coroutine
async def task():
    # do things...
```

This syntax defines an awaitable, which is a unit of execution that can be awaited, e.g. waited for.

A program can wait on an awaitable asynchronous task to complete using the `await` expression; for example:

```
...
# create and schedule the coroutine, then wait
await task()
```

This line will do two things:

- Create a coroutine and schedule it for execution.
- Yield execution until the coroutine returns.

It is also possible to define a collection of coroutines, such as in a list.

For example:

```
...
# create a list of coroutines
task_list = [task() for _ in range(10)]
```

This will create a list of ten coroutines, instead of calling the `task()` coroutine ten times.

We can await on each coroutine in turn. Alternatively we can call the `asyncio.gather()` function to execute a collection of coroutines and wait for them all to complete.

This can be achieved by passing multiple coroutine to the `asyncio.gather()` function directly.

For example:

```
...
# execute tasks and wait for them to complete
asyncio.gather(task(), task(), task())
```

Alternately, we can provide a collection of coroutines to the function and unpack them using the star (*) operator.

For example:

```
...
# create a list of coroutines
task_list = [task() for _ in range(10)]
# execute tasks and wait for them to complete
asyncio.gather(*task_list)
```

Coroutines can only be awaited with other coroutines, and all coroutines must run within an asyncio event loop.

We can create and start an asyncio event loop by calling the `asyncio.run()` function and create the coroutine to run as the entry point to our asyncio program.

For example:

```
...
# start the asyncio runtime
asyncio.run(main())
```

This will create the event loop runtime required to support the scheduling and execution of coroutines.

Now that we know the basics of asyncio, let's look at developing a worked example of an asyncio program.

16.3   Example Of An Asyncio Program

We can explore how to develop an asyncio program that executes a custom coroutine.

First, we can define a task function as a coroutine using the `async` def expression.

The task will simulate an I/O operation for a moment and print a message.

We must await the sleep operation which yields control to any other coroutines in the runtime.

```
# task that blocks for a moment and prints a message
async def task():
    # block for a moment
    await asyncio.sleep(1)
    # display a message
    print('This is coming from another coroutine')
```

We can then create the coroutine and await for it to complete.

```
...
# run task and wait for it to complete
await task()
```

This can be performed in a second custom coroutine that is used to drive the program called the main coroutine.

```
# demonstrate executing a task in a coroutine
async def main():
    print('Waiting for the new coroutine to finish...')
    # run task and wait for it to complete
    await task()
```

Finally, we can start the asyncio event loop and run the main coroutine.

```
...
# start the event loop
asyncio.run(main())
```

Tying this together, the complete example of executing a task in a coroutine using asyncio is listed below.

```
# SuperFastPython.com
# example of running a function in a new coroutine
import asyncio
```

```
# task that blocks for a moment and prints a message
async def task():
    # block for a moment
    await asyncio.sleep(1)
    # display a message
    print('This is coming from another coroutine')

# demonstrate executing a task in a coroutine
async def main():
    print('Waiting for the new coroutine to finish...')
    # run task and wait for it to complete
    await task()

# start the event loop
asyncio.run(main())
```

Running the example starts the asyncio event loop, then creates the `main()` coroutine and schedules it for execution.

The `main()` coroutine runs and prints a message, it then schedules the `task()` coroutine for execution and waits for it to be done.

The `task()` coroutine runs and schedules the `sleep()` coroutine to run and awaits it to complete.

The sleep is completed and the `task()` coroutine resumes, prints a message, then terminates.

The `main()` coroutine resumes and terminates and the program exits.

This highlights how we can define new custom coroutines and how we can create, execute, and await coroutines in an asyncio program.

```
Waiting for the new coroutine to finish...
This is coming from another coroutine
```

16.4   Further Reading

This section lists helpful additional resources on the topic.

- Python Concurrent Execution.
  https://docs.python.org/3/library/concurrency.html
- `threading` – Thread-based parallelism.
  https://docs.python.org/3/library/threading.html
- `multiprocessing` – Process-based parallelism.
  https://docs.python.org/3/library/multiprocessing.html
- `concurrent.futures` – Launching parallel tasks.
  https://docs.python.org/3/library/concurrent.futures.html
- `asyncio` – Asynchronous I/O.
  https://docs.python.org/3/library/asyncio.html

16.5   Takeaways

You now know the basics of coroutines and asyncio.

Specifically, you know:

- What is asyncio and how does it relate to threading and multi-processing.
- How to use the async and await syntax.
- How to define, create, and run custom coroutines in an asyncio program.

16.5.1   Next

In the next tutorial, we will explore how to benchmark asyncio programs using the `loop.time()` method.

Chapter 17

Benchmarking Asyncio With `loop.time()`

You can benchmark Python code using the `loop.time()` method on the asyncio event loop.

The asyncio event loop maintains an internal monotonic timer. It is mostly used for managing timeouts and delays. We can retrieve the current time maintained by asyncio via the `loop.time()` method.

In this tutorial, you will discover how to benchmark asyncio programs using the `loop.time()` method.

After completing this tutorial, you will know:

- What is the `loop.time()` method and its strengths and limitations when used for benchmarking.
- How to check the properties of the `loop.time()` method such as whether stops during a sleep or blocking call.
- How to use the `loop.time()` method to benchmark statements, coroutines, and asyncio programs.

Let's get started.

17.1   What Is `loop.time()`

The asyncio event loop maintains an internal timer.

This timer is monotonic, meaning that whenever the time is retrieved it is always equal to or greater than the last time that was retrieved. The underlying clock cannot be adjusted backward in time via time synchronization or daylight savings.

We can access the time maintained by the event loop via the `time()` method on the event loop object.

> Return the current time, as a float value, according to the event loop's internal monotonic clock.

– Asyncio Event Loop.

This means that we must first retrieve the event loop object, and then call the `time()` method to get the time.

We can get the object for the current event loop via the `asyncio.get_running_loop()` function.

For example:

```
...
# get the event loop
loop = asyncio.get_running_loop()
# get the current event loop time
time = loop.time()
```

If we want to retrieve the time many times in our program, such as during benchmarking, we could reduce this to a single compound statement.

For example:

```
...
# get the current event loop time
time = asyncio.get_running_loop().time()
```

The `loop.time()` method is implemented using the `monotonic()` function in the `time` module.

Recall that the `time.monotonic()` function provides a timer that uses a system-wide monotonic clock that is not adjustable.

It is used in the Python standard library generally for timeouts and delays, much as the `loop.time()` method is used in the asyncio event loop.

The comment for the default implementation of the `time()` method is telling.

It reminds us that the implementation may differ from event loop to event loop, and we should not rely on the default properties of `time.monotonic()`, e.g. the precision, the clock used, and the fact that it's not adjusted.

Now that we know about the `loop.time()` method, let's look at how we can use it to benchmark our asyncio programs.

17.2 How To Benchmark

We can use the `loop.time()` method to benchmark asyncio programs.

There are perhaps 3 case studies we may want to consider, they are:

1. Benchmarking a statement.
2. Benchmarking a coroutine.
3. Benchmarking an asyncio program.

Let's look at how we can benchmark using the `loop.time()` method.

17.2.1 How To Benchmark A Statement

We can use the `loop.time()` method to benchmark arbitrary statements.

The procedure is as follows:

1. Record `loop.time()` before the statement.
2. Execute the statement.
3. Record `loop.time()` after the statement.

4. Subtract start time from after time to give duration.
5. Report the duration using `print()`.

For example:

```
...
# record start time
time_start = asyncio.get_running_loop().time()
# execute the statement
  ...
# record end time
time_end = asyncio.get_running_loop().time()
# calculate the duration
time_duration = time_end - time_start
# report the duration
print(f'Took {time_duration:.3f} seconds')
```

17.2.2   How To Benchmark A Coroutine

We can use the `loop.time()` method to benchmark arbitrary asyncio coroutines.

The procedure is as follows:

1. Record `loop.time()` before the coroutine.
2. Await the coroutine.
3. Record `loop.time()` after the coroutine.
4. Subtract start time from after time to give duration.
5. Report the duration using `print()`.

For example:

```
...
# record start time
time_start = asyncio.get_running_loop().time()
# await the coroutine
  ...
# record end time
time_end = asyncio.get_running_loop().time()
# calculate the duration
```

```
time_duration = time_end - time_start
# report the duration
print(f'Took {time_duration:.3f} seconds')
```

17.2.3   How To Benchmark An Asyncio Program

We can use the `loop.time()` method to benchmark arbitrary asyncio programs.

Typically, the entry point to an asyncio program is a coroutine called `main()`. We can add the benchmarking code to the beginning and end of this coroutine.

This coroutine can then be created and passed to the `asyncio.run()` function to start the event loop and run the asyncio program.

The procedure is as follows:

1. Record `loop.time()` at the beginning of the `main()` coroutine.
2. Run the body of the `main()` coroutine.
3. Record `loop.time()` at the end of the `main()` coroutine.
4. Subtract start time from after time to give duration.
5. Report the duration using `print()`.

For example:

```
...

# define main coroutine
async def main():
    # record start time
    time_start = asyncio.get_running_loop().time()
    # execute the program
    ...
    # record end time
    time_end = asyncio.get_running_loop().time()
    # calculate the duration
    time_duration = time_end - time_start
    # report the duration
    print(f'Took {time_duration:.3f} seconds')
```

```
# start the event loop
asyncio.run(main())
```

Now that we know how to benchmark code using `loop.time()`, let's look at some worked examples.

17.3 Example Of Benchmarking A Statement

We can explore how to benchmark a statement using `loop.time()` in an asyncio program with a worked example.

In this example, we will define a statement that creates a list of 100 million squared integers in a list comprehension, which should take a number of seconds.

```
...
# execute the statement
data = [i*i for i in range(100000000)]
```

We will then surround this statement with benchmarking code.

Firstly, we will record the start time using the `loop.time()` method.

```
...
# record start time
time_start = asyncio.get_running_loop().time()
```

Afterward, we will record the end time, calculate the overall execution duration, and report the result.

```
...
# record end time
time_end = asyncio.get_running_loop().time()
# calculate the duration
time_duration = time_end - time_start
# report the duration
print(f'Took {time_duration:.3f} seconds')
```

Tying this together, the complete example is listed below.

```
# SuperFastPython.com
# example of benchmarking a statement with loop.time()
import asyncio

# define coroutine
async def main():
    # record start time
    time_start = asyncio.get_running_loop().time()
    # execute the statement
    data = [i*i for i in range(100000000)]
    # record end time
    time_end = asyncio.get_running_loop().time()
    # calculate the duration
    time_duration = time_end - time_start
    # report the duration
    print(f'Took {time_duration:.3f} seconds')

# run the coroutine
asyncio.run(main())
```

Running the example first starts the asyncio event loop and runs the `main()` coroutine.

The `main()` coroutine runs and records the start time using the event loop time.

Next, the statement is executed, in this case creating a list of 100 million squared integers.

The end time is then recorded, using the event loop time.

The difference between the two recorded times is calculated, providing the statement execution duration in seconds.

Finally, the result is reported, truncated to three decimal places (milliseconds).

In this case, we can see that the statement took about 5.139 seconds to complete.

Note, the results on your system may differ.

This highlights how we can benchmark a statement in an asyncio program using the `loop.time()` method.

```
Took 5.139 seconds
```

Next, let's explore an example of benchmarking a coroutine using the `loop.time()` method.

17.4   Example Of Benchmarking A Coroutine

We can explore how to benchmark an asyncio coroutine using `loop.time()` with a worked example.

In this example, we will define a coroutine that creates a list of 100 million squared integers in a list comprehension, which should take a number of seconds.

```
# our work coroutine
async def work():
    # do some CPU bound work
    data = [i*i for i in range(100000000)]
```

We will then await this coroutine, and surround the call with benchmarking code.

Firstly, we will record the start time using the `loop.time()` method.
```
...
# record start time
time_start = asyncio.get_running_loop().time()
```

Afterward, we will record the end time, calculate the overall execution duration, and report the result.
```
...
# record end time
time_end = asyncio.get_running_loop().time()
# calculate the duration
```

```
time_duration = time_end - time_start
# report the duration
print(f'Took {time_duration:.3f} seconds')
```

Tying this together, the complete example is listed below.

```
# SuperFastPython.com
# example of benchmarking a coroutine
import asyncio

# our work coroutine
async def work():
    # do some CPU bound work
    data = [i*i for i in range(100000000)]

# define coroutine
async def main():
    # record start time
    time_start = asyncio.get_running_loop().time()
    # suspend and await the coroutine
    await work()
    # record end time
    time_end = asyncio.get_running_loop().time()
    # calculate the duration
    time_duration = time_end - time_start
    # report the duration
    print(f'Took {time_duration:.3f} seconds')

# run the coroutine
asyncio.run(main())
```

Running the example first starts the asyncio event loop and runs the main() coroutine.

The main() coroutine runs and records the start time using the event loop time.

Next, the work() coroutine is awaited. This suspends the main()

coroutine and executes the `work()` coroutine, in this case creating a list of 100 million squared integers.

The `main()` coroutine resumes and the end time is then recorded using the event loop time.

The difference between the two recorded times is calculated, providing the coroutine execution duration in seconds.

Finally, the result is reported, truncated to three decimal places (milliseconds).

In this case, we can see that the function took about 6.273 seconds to complete.

Note, the results on your system may differ.

This highlights how we can benchmark an asyncio coroutine using the `loop.time()` method.

```
Took 6.273 seconds
```

Next, let's confirm that benchmarking with `loop.time()` includes await times.

17.5   Example Of Checking Await Time

A concern when using the `loop.time()` method for benchmarking is whether the recorded interval includes await times.

Generally, the `loop.time()` method internally uses the `time.monotonic()` function which uses an internal clock that is not suspended when the calling coroutine, thread, and process is blocked.

Nevertheless, this behavior is not documented and we can confirm it with a worked example.

In this case, we will define a coroutine that suspends by awaiting `asyncio.sleep()` for one second.

```
# our work coroutine
async def work():
    # sleep a moment
    await asyncio.sleep(1)
```

We will then benchmark this coroutine for one second and expect that the duration is about one second.

```
# define coroutine
async def main():
    # record start time
    time_start = asyncio.get_running_loop().time()
    # await the target coroutine
    await work()
    # record end time
    time_end = asyncio.get_running_loop().time()
    # calculate the duration
    time_duration = time_end - time_start
    # report the duration
    print(f'Took {time_duration:.3f} seconds')
```

Tying this together, the complete example is listed below.

```
# SuperFastPython.com
# example of benchmarking a coroutine that awaits
import asyncio

# our work coroutine
async def work():
    # sleep a moment
    await asyncio.sleep(1)

# define coroutine
async def main():
    # record start time
    time_start = asyncio.get_running_loop().time()
    # await the target coroutine
    await work()
```

```
# record end time
time_end = asyncio.get_running_loop().time()
# calculate the duration
time_duration = time_end - time_start
# report the duration
print(f'Took {time_duration:.3f} seconds')

# run the coroutine
asyncio.run(main())
```

Running the example first starts the asyncio event loop and runs the main() coroutine.

The main() coroutine runs and records the start time using the event loop time.

Next, the work() coroutine is awaited. This suspends the main() coroutine and executes the work() coroutine, in this case suspending and awaiting asyncio.sleep() for one second. The work() coroutine then resumes and terminates.

The main() coroutine resumes and the end time is then recorded using the event loop time.

The difference between the two recorded times is calculated, providing the coroutine execution duration in seconds.

Finally, the result is reported, truncated to three decimal places (milliseconds).

In this case, we can see that the function took about 1.005 seconds to complete. This matches our expectation of about one second.

Note, the results on your system may differ.

This highlights that using loop.time() for benchmarking in asyncio programs includes await times, and that the clock used by the event loop is not suspended when the program sleeps.

```
Took 1.005 seconds
```

Next, let's confirm that when the loop.time() method is used for benchmarking, that it includes time when the thread that is managing the event loop is blocked.

17.6 Example Of Checking Blocking Time

Another concern with using `loop.time()` is that we are not sure if the underlying clock will be suspended if the thread in which the event loop is running is blocked.

For example, if the thread is paused with a call to `time.sleep()`, this will block both the main thread and the event loop.

```
# our work coroutine
async def work():
    # sleep a moment
    time.sleep(1)
```

We suspect that the underlying event loop clock will not be suspended, but we can confirm this with a worked example.

The complete example is listed below.

```
# SuperFastPython.com
# example of benchmarking a blocking coroutine
import asyncio

# our work coroutine
async def work():
    # sleep a moment
    time.sleep(1)

# define coroutine
async def main():
    # record start time
    time_start = asyncio.get_running_loop().time()
    # await the target coroutine
    await work()
```

```
    # record end time
    time_end = asyncio.get_running_loop().time()
    # calculate the duration
    time_duration = time_end - time_start
    # report the duration
    print(f'Took {time_duration:.3f} seconds')

# run the coroutine
asyncio.run(main())
```

Running the example first starts the asyncio event loop and runs the `main()` coroutine.

The `main()` coroutine runs and records the start time using the event loop time.

Next, the `work()` coroutine is awaited. This suspends the `main()` coroutine and executes the `work()` coroutine, in this case blocking the event loop and the current thread with a call to `time.sleep()`. The `work()` coroutine then resumes and terminates.

The `main()` coroutine resumes and the end time is then recorded using the event loop time.

The difference between the two recorded times is calculated, providing the coroutine execution duration in seconds.

Finally, the result is reported, truncated to three decimal places (milliseconds).

In this case, we can see that the function took about 1.005 seconds to complete. This matches the expectation of about one second.

Note, the results on your system may differ.

This highlights that using `loop.time()` for benchmarking in asyncio programs includes calls that block the event loop and the current thread.

```
Took 1.005 seconds
```

17.7 Further Reading

This section lists helpful additional resources on the topic.

- Asyncio Event Loop.
  https://docs.python.org/3/library/asyncio-eventloop.html
- `asyncio` – Asynchronous I/O.
  https://docs.python.org/3/library/asyncio.html
- `time` – Time access and conversions.
  https://docs.python.org/3/library/time.html

17.8 Takeaways

You now know how to benchmark asyncio programs using the `loop.time()` method.

Specifically, you know:

- What is the `loop.time()` method and its strengths and limitations when used for benchmarking.
- How to check the properties of the `loop.time()` method such as whether stops during a sleep or blocking call.
- How to use the `loop.time()` method to benchmark statements, coroutines, and asyncio programs.

17.8.1 Next

In the next tutorial, we will explore how to develop a benchmark helper coroutine.

Chapter 18

Benchmark Helper Coroutine

You can develop a helper coroutine to record and report the overall execution time of coroutines and tasks in asyncio programs.

The helper coroutine can be implemented using a try-finally structure so that it is still able to report the overall benchmark execution time even if the target task fails with an exception or is canceled.

In this tutorial, you will discover how to develop a helper coroutine to benchmark asyncio tasks and coroutines.

After completing this tutorial, you will know:

- How to use helper coroutines for benchmarking target coroutines.
- How to develop a helper asyncio coroutine for benchmarking coroutines.
- How the helper benchmark coroutine behaves when run in the background and when canceled.

Let's get started.

18.1 Need A Benchmark Helper Coroutine

We have seen in a previous chapter how to develop a benchmark helper function.

The helper function can be used to execute arbitrary functions, with an arbitrary number of arguments and a possible return value.

The benchmark helper function cannot be used to benchmark coroutines in asyncio programs.

The reason is because the helper function executes a target function. Whereas a target coroutine is not executed, instead it is scheduled for execution in the event loop and is awaited.

Attempting to benchmark a coroutine using the helper function will result in an error.

Additionally, once a coroutine is scheduled as a task, it may be canceled at any time. We may want to stop and report the benchmark once the coroutine is done, even if it is canceled or fails with an unhandled exception.

Therefore, we need to develop a helper coroutine specifically for benchmarking a target coroutine in asyncio programs.

18.2 How To Develop A Benchmark Coroutine

We can develop a helper coroutine to automatically benchmark our code.

Our coroutine can take an awaitable to run. This could be a created coroutine object or an instance of an `asyncio.Task`.

For example:

```
# benchmark coroutine
async def benchmark(awaitable):
    # ...
```

We want our **benchmark()** to be a coroutine so that we can await it and the target awaitable will execute.

Recall that when we call a coroutine we are in fact creating an instance of a coroutine object that is an awaitable type that can be awaited via the **await** expression.

We don't need to provide any arguments to the target, we can assume that the awaitable has been created and is provided ready to be executed.

Our coroutine can then record the start time, await the target awaitable, record the end time, and report the overall duration. We will use the **time.perf_counter()** time function, preferred for benchmarking.

Importantly, we need to handle the case that the target is canceled for some reason, or perhaps terminated due to an exception.

Recall that a task can be canceled at any time, even by the event loop when it is shut down.

We can handle this case by awaiting the target awaitable within a try-finally structure and recording and reporting the duration in the finally block.

For example:

```
...
# record start time
time_start = perf_counter()
try:
    # await the target
    await awaitable
finally:
    # record end time
    time_end = perf_counter()
```

```
# calculate the duration
time_duration = time_end - time_start
# report the duration
print(f'Took {time_duration:.3f} seconds')
```

Tying this together with a helper coroutine for benchmarking arbitrary asyncio tasks and coroutines is listed below.

```
# benchmark coroutine
async def benchmark(awaitable):
    # record start time
    time_start = perf_counter()
    try:
        # await the target
        await awaitable
    finally:
        # record end time
        time_end = perf_counter()
        # calculate the duration
        time_duration = time_end - time_start
        # report the duration
        print(f'Took {time_duration:.3f} seconds')
```

To benchmark a coroutine we can create a coroutine and pass it as an argument then await the benchmark() coroutine directly.

For example:

```
...
# benchmark a coroutine
await benchmark(work())
```

To benchmark an asyncio.Task, we can create the task directly or via a TaskGroup then pass it to the benchmark() coroutine and await it.

For example:

```
...
# benchmark a task
await benchmark(task)
```

Now that we know how to develop a helper benchmark coroutine, let's look at how we might use it.

18.3   Example   Of   Benchmarking   A Coroutine

We can explore an example of benchmarking the execution time of a coroutine using our helper.

In this case, we will define a coroutine that takes a long time performing a CPU-bound task. We will then execute this task via our `benchmark()` coroutine developed above and report the overall execution time.

Firstly, we can define a coroutine that runs a long time. Our task will prepare a list of 100 million squared integers.

The `work()` coroutine below implements this.

```
# task to benchmark
async def work():
    # create a large list
    data = [i*i for i in range(100000000)]
```

The `main()` coroutine will then execute this task via our `benchmark()` coroutine developed above.

```
# main coroutine
async def main():
    # report a message
    print('Main starting')
    # benchmark the execution of our task
    await benchmark(work())
    # report a message
    print('Main done')
```

This will run our task and report the overall execution time for the task.

Tying this together, the complete example is listed below.

```python
# SuperFastPython.com
# example of benchmarking a coroutine with a helper
from time import perf_counter
import asyncio

# benchmark coroutine
async def benchmark(awaitable):
    # record start time
    time_start = perf_counter()
    try:
        # await the target
        await awaitable
    finally:
        # record end time
        time_end = perf_counter()
        # calculate the duration
        time_duration = time_end - time_start
        # report the duration
        print(f'Took {time_duration:.3f} seconds')

# task to benchmark
async def work():
    # create a large list
    data = [i*i for i in range(100000000)]

# main coroutine
async def main():
    # report a message
    print('Main starting')
    # benchmark the execution of our task
    await benchmark(work())
    # report a message
    print('Main done')

# start the event loop
```

```
asyncio.run(main())
```

Running the example first starts the event loop and runs the **main()** coroutine.

The **main()** coroutine runs and reports a start message.

It then suspends and awaits the **benchmark()** coroutine and passes in an instance of our **work()** coroutine.

The **benchmark()** coroutine runs and records the start time. It then awaits the passed-in coroutine object.

The **work()** coroutine runs and creates a list of 100 million squared integers. This blocks the event loop.

The **work()** coroutine terminates and the **benchmark()** coroutine resumes. It records the end time, calculates the duration, and reports the duration in seconds.

In this case, we can see that the **work()** coroutine took about 6.178 seconds to complete.

Note, the results on your system may differ.

The **benchmark()** coroutine terminates and the **main()** coroutine resumes and reports a final message before the program exits.

This highlights how we can benchmark the execution time of a coroutine using our helper coroutine.

```
Main starting
Took 6.178 seconds
Main done
```

Next, let's look at how we might benchmark an asyncio task.

18.4   Example Of Benchmarking An Asyncio Task

We can explore how to benchmark the execution time of an asyncio task using our `benchmark()` helper coroutine.

In this case, we can update the above example to first create and schedule the `work()` coroutine as an `asyncio.Task`, then pass the `asyncio.Task` instance to the `benchmark()` coroutine.

```
...
# create the task
task = asyncio.create_task(work())
# benchmark the execution of our task
await benchmark(task)
```

The `benchmark()` helper coroutine can take any awaitable, such as a coroutine object or an `asyncio.Task`, so the target task will be awaited and its execution time reported as expected.

Tying this together, the complete example is listed below.

```
# SuperFastPython.com
# example of benchmarking a task with a helper
from time import perf_counter
import asyncio

# benchmark coroutine
async def benchmark(awaitable):
    # record start time
    time_start = perf_counter()
    try:
        # await the target
        await awaitable
    finally:
        # record end time
        time_end = perf_counter()
        # calculate the duration
        time_duration = time_end - time_start
```

```
        # report the duration
        print(f'Took {time_duration:.3f} seconds')

# task to benchmark
async def work():
    # create a large list
    data = [i*i for i in range(100000000)]

# main coroutine
async def main():
    # report a message
    print('Main starting')
    # create the task
    task = asyncio.create_task(work())
    # benchmark the execution of our task
    await benchmark(task)
    # report a message
    print('Main done')

# start the event loop
asyncio.run(main())
```

Running the example first starts the event loop and runs the `main()` coroutine.

The `main()` coroutine runs and reports a start message.

It then creates and schedules a new `asyncio.Task` instance and passes it a `work()` coroutine instance.

The `main()` coroutine then suspends and awaits the `benchmark()` coroutine and passes in an instance of our task instance.

The `benchmark()` coroutine runs and records the start time. It then awaits the passed-in `asyncio.Task` object.

The `work()` coroutine runs and creates a list of 100 million squared integers. This blocks the event loop.

The `work()` coroutine terminates and the `benchmark()` coroutine resumes. It records the end time, calculates the duration, and reports the duration in seconds.

In this case, we can see that the work() coroutine took about 6.384 seconds to complete.

Note, the results on your system may differ.

The benchmark() coroutine terminates and the main() coroutine resumes and reports a final message before the program exits.

This highlights how we can benchmark the execution time of an asyncio.Task using our helper coroutine.

```
Main starting
Took 6.384 seconds
Main done
```

Next let's look at benchmarking a coroutine as a background task.

18.5 Example Of Benchmarking In A Background Task

We can explore an example of benchmarking an asyncio coroutine as a background task.

In this case, we can update the above example to benchmark our work() coroutine directly but to do so as a background task.

This means that the benchmark() coroutine will be scheduled and executed as an asyncio.Task while the main() coroutine proceeds with other tasks, in this case, a long sleep.

```
...
# create a task to perform the benchmarking
task = asyncio.create_task(benchmark(work()))
# wait around doing other things
await asyncio.sleep(8)
```

Tying this together, the complete example is listed below.

```
# SuperFastPython.com
# example of benchmarking a background task with helper
from time import perf_counter
import asyncio

# benchmark coroutine
async def benchmark(awaitable):
    # record start time
    time_start = perf_counter()
    try:
        # await the target
        await awaitable
    finally:
        # record end time
        time_end = perf_counter()
        # calculate the duration
        time_duration = time_end - time_start
        # report the duration
        print(f'Took {time_duration:.3f} seconds')

# task to benchmark
async def work():
    # create a large list
    data = [i*i for i in range(100000000)]

# main coroutine
async def main():
    # report a message
    print('Main starting')
    # create a task to perform the benchmarking
    task = asyncio.create_task(benchmark(work()))
    # wait around doing other things
    await asyncio.sleep(8)
    # report a message
    print('Main done')
```

```
# start the event loop
asyncio.run(main())
```

The `main()` coroutine runs and reports a start message.

It then creates and schedules a new `asyncio.Task` instance and passes it a `benchmark()` coroutine that in turn is passed an instance of our `work()` coroutine.

The `main()` coroutine then suspends and sleeps for 8 seconds, enough time for our 6-second CPU-bound task to complete

The `benchmark()` background task runs and records the start time. It then awaits the passed-in coroutine object.

The `work()` coroutine runs and creates a list of 100 million squared integers. This blocks the event loop.

The `work()` coroutine terminates and the `benchmark()` task resumes. It records the end time, calculates the duration, and reports the duration in seconds.

In this case, we can see that the `work()` coroutine took about 6.018 seconds to complete. The `benchmark()` coroutine terminates.

Note, the results on your system may differ.

Later, the `main()` coroutine finishes its sleep and resumes. It reports a final message and then exits.

This highlights how we can benchmark the execution time of a coroutine using our helper coroutine in the background.

```
Main starting
Took 6.018 seconds
Main done
```

Next, let's look at what happens if the target awaitable that is being benchmarked is canceled.

18.6 Example Of Benchmarking A Task That Is Canceled

We can explore an example of the target coroutine being canceled while the execution time is being benchmarked.

In this case, we will update the above example so that the target task can be canceled, e.g., is awaiting a call to `asyncio.sleep()`.

```
# task to benchmark
async def work():
    # create a large list
    await asyncio.sleep(5)
```

We will then benchmark our `work()` coroutine in the background, but update the `main()` sleep so that it does not give enough time for the `work()` task to complete, e.g. 3 seconds instead of 5 or more seconds.

```
...
# create a task to perform the benchmarking
task = asyncio.create_task(benchmark(work()))
# wait around doing other things
await asyncio.sleep(3)
```

This will mean that the `main()` coroutine will exit and shut down the event loop while the `benchmark()` coroutine is awaiting the `work()` coroutine, canceling both.

Tying this together, the complete example is listed below.

```
# SuperFastPython.com
# example of benchmarking a canceled task with helper
from time import perf_counter
import asyncio

# benchmark coroutine
async def benchmark(awaitable):
    # record start time
    time_start = perf_counter()
```

```
    try:
        # await the target
        await awaitable
    finally:
        # record end time
        time_end = perf_counter()
        # calculate the duration
        time_duration = time_end - time_start
        # report the duration
        print(f'Took {time_duration:.3f} seconds')

# task to benchmark
async def work():
    # create a large list
    await asyncio.sleep(5)

# main coroutine
async def main():
    # report a message
    print('Main starting')
    # create a task to perform the benchmarking
    task = asyncio.create_task(benchmark(work()))
    # wait around doing other things
    await asyncio.sleep(3)
    # report a message
    print('Main done')

# start the event loop
asyncio.run(main())
```

The `main()` coroutine runs and reports a start message.

It then creates and schedules a new `asyncio.Task` instance and passes it a `benchmark()` coroutine that in turn is passed an instance of our `work()` coroutine.

The `main()` coroutine then suspends and sleeps for 3 seconds, not enough time for our 5-second `work()` coroutine to complete

The `benchmark()` background task runs and records the start time. It then awaits the passed-in coroutine object.

The `work()` coroutine runs and sleeps for 5 seconds.

The `main()` coroutine resumes and exits. This shuts down the asyncio event loop and cancels all running tasks.

The `work()` coroutine is canceled, raising a `CancelledError` exception and terminating.

The `CancelledError` exception is raised in the `benchmark()` coroutine which exits, first executing the finally block. This records the end time, calculates the duration, and reports the duration in seconds.

We can see that the `work()` task execution time is trimmed to about 3.003 seconds, instead of the expected 5 seconds.

Note, the results on your system may differ.

This highlights how we can still report the benchmark execution time of coroutines and tasks that are canceled while being benchmarked.

```
Main starting
Main done
Took 3.003 seconds
```

18.7 Further Reading

This section lists helpful additional resources on the topic.

- `asyncio` – Asynchronous I/O.
  https://docs.python.org/3/library/asyncio.html
- `time` – Time access and conversions.
  https://docs.python.org/3/library/time.html

18.8 Takeaways

You now know how to develop a helper coroutine to benchmark asyncio tasks and coroutines.

Specifically, you know:

- How to use helper coroutines for benchmarking target coroutines.
- How to develop a helper asyncio coroutine for benchmarking coroutines.
- How the helper benchmark coroutine behaves when run in the background and when canceled.

18.8.1   Next

In the next tutorial, we will explore how to develop a benchmark asynchronous context manager.

Chapter 19

Benchmark Asynchronous Context Manager

You can develop a custom asynchronous context manager to automatically benchmark asyncio code in Python.

An asynchronous context manager is a context manager that can be suspended in asyncio when it is entered and exited. We can wrap code that we wish to automatically benchmark using a custom asynchronous context manager.

In this tutorial, you will discover how to benchmark asyncio code using an asynchronous context manager.

After completing this tutorial, you will know:

- How to develop an asynchronous context manager to benchmark coroutines and tasks.
- How to use an asynchronous context manager for benchmarking in asyncio.

Let's get started.

19.1 Need A Benchmark Asynchronous Context Manager

We have seen in a previous chapter how to develop a benchmark context manager.

The benchmark context manager can be used to execute an arbitrary block of code and will automatically record the start time and end time, then calculate and report the overall execution time for the code block.

The problem is, we cannot use the benchmark context manager to benchmark blocks of code in an asyncio program.

Specifically, we cannot use await expressions within a context manager, meaning we cannot benchmark code that suspends and waits for other coroutines and tasks. Attempting to do so will result in an error.

Instead, we need to develop a context manager that supports awaiting within the body. This is called an asynchronous context manager.

19.2 How To Develop An Asynchronous Context Manager

We can hide manual benchmarking of asyncio code in an asynchronous context manager.

An asynchronous context manager is just like a regular (synchronous) context manager, except it is able to be suspended in the entry, exit methods and within the body.

It has a different interface, requiring a Python object that implements the `__aenter__`() and `__aexit__`() methods.

> An asynchronous context manager is a context manager that is able to suspend execution in its `__aenter__` and `__aexit__` methods.

– Asynchronous Context Managers, Data Model.

The __aenter__ and __aexit__ methods are defined as coroutines and are awaited by the caller.

This is achieved using the **async with** expression.

We can define a new class that implements a constructor __init__() and the __aenter__() and __aexit__() coroutines.

The __init__() constructor can take a name argument for the benchmark case and store it in an object attribute.

For example:

```
# constructor
def __init__(self, name):
    # store the name of this benchmark
    self.name = name
```

The __aenter__() coroutine can initialize the start time and store it in an object attribute.

We will use the time.perf_counter() time function, preferred for benchmarking.

For example:

```
...
# enter the async context manager
async def __aenter__(self):
    # record the start time
    self.time_start = perf_counter()
    # return this object
    return self
```

The __aexit__() coroutine must take some standard arguments.

It will record the end time, calculate and store the duration, and report the calculated duration along with the name of the benchmark case.

```
...
# exit the async context manager
```

```
async def __aexit__(self, exc_type, exc, tb):
    # record the end time
    self.time_end = perf_counter()
    # calculate the duration
    self.duration = self.time_end - self.time_start
    # report the duration
    print(f'{self.name} took {self.duration:.3f} s')
    # do not suppress any exception
    return False
```

Tying this together, we can define a Benchmark asynchronous context manager below.

```
# benchmark asynchronous context manager
class Benchmark:
    # constructor
    def __init__(self, name):
        # store the name of this benchmark
        self.name = name

    # enter the async context manager
    async def __aenter__(self):
        # record the start time
        self.time_start = perf_counter()
        # return this object
        return self

    # exit the async context manager
    async def __aexit__(self, exc_type, exc, tb):
        # record the end time
        self.time_end = perf_counter()
        # calculate the duration
        self.duration = self.time_end - self.time_start
        # report the duration
        print(f'{self.name} took {self.duration:.3f} s')
        # do not suppress any exception
        return False
```

We can then use it by creating an instance of the **Benchmark** class within the **async with** expression and then list any code within the context we wish to benchmark.

For example:

```
...
# create the benchmark context
async with Benchmark('Task'):
    # run the task
    await coro()
```

The code within the context manager will run as per normal, and once finished, the total execution time will be reported automatically.

Now that we know how to develop and use a benchmark context manager, let's look at some examples.

19.3 Example Of Benchmarking A Coroutine

We can explore how to use our **Benchmark** asynchronous context manager to benchmark the execution time of a custom coroutine.

In this example, we will define a coroutine that blocks the event loop with a CPU-bound task.

The coroutine creates a list of 100 million squared integers in a list comprehension.

For example:

```
# task to benchmark
async def work():
    # create a large list
    data = [i*i for i in range(100000000)]
```

We can then await this comprehension within the **Benchmark** asynchronous context manager to have the execution time automatically recorded and reported.

For example:

```python
# benchmark the execution of our task
async with Benchmark('work()'):
    await work()
```

Tying this together, the complete example is listed below.

```python
# SuperFastPython.com
# example of benchmarking a coro with async context mgmr
from time import perf_counter
import asyncio

# benchmark asynchronous context manager
class Benchmark:
    # constructor
    def __init__(self, name):
        # store the name of this benchmark
        self.name = name
    # enter the async context manager
    async def __aenter__(self):
        # record the start time
        self.time_start = perf_counter()
        # return this object
        return self

    # exit the async context manager
    async def __aexit__(self, exc_type, exc, tb):
        # record the end time
        self.time_end = perf_counter()
        # calculate the duration
        self.duration = self.time_end - self.time_start
        # report the duration
        print(f'{self.name} took {self.duration:.3f} s')
        # do not suppress any exception
        return False

# task to benchmark
```

```
async def work():
    # create a large list
    data = [i*i for i in range(100000000)]

# main coroutine
async def main():
    # report a message
    print('Main starting')
    # benchmark the execution of our task
    async with Benchmark('work()'):
        await work()
    # report a message
    print('Main done')

# start the event loop
asyncio.run(main())
```

Running the example first starts the asyncio event loop and runs the main() coroutine.

The main() coroutine runs and reports a message.

It then creates the Benchmark asynchronous context manager via the async with expression and provides the name "work()", which is stored in an object attribute.

The main() coroutine suspends and the context manager is entered, automatically awaiting the __aenter__() coroutine where the start time is recorded in an object attribute.

The task() coroutine is then awaited in the body of the context manager and the list is created.

Finally, the asynchronous context manager is exited, automatically awaiting the __aexit__() method, recording the end time, calculating the duration, and reporting it to standard out.

In this case, we can see that the task() coroutine took about 6.340 seconds to complete.

Note, the results on your system may differ.

This highlights how we can benchmark arbitrary asyncio code using a custom asynchronous context manager.

```
Main starting
work() took 6.340 s
Main done
```

Next, let's take a look at how we might benchmark an asyncio task instead of a coroutine.

19.4   Example Of Benchmarking An Asyncio Task

We can explore how to use our `Benchmark` asynchronous context manager to benchmark the execution time of an asyncio `Task`.

In this case, we can update the above example to first create an `asyncio.Task` to run our `work()` coroutine, then await the new task within the `Benchmark` asynchronous context manager.

```
...
# create the task
task = asyncio.create_task(work())
# benchmark the execution of our task
async with Benchmark('work()'):
    await task
```

Tying this together, the complete example is listed below.

```
# SuperFastPython.com
# example of benchmarking a task with async context mgmr
from time import perf_counter
import asyncio

# benchmark asynchronous context manager
class Benchmark:
    # constructor
    def __init__(self, name):
```

```
        # store the name of this benchmark
        self.name = name
    # enter the async context manager
    async def __aenter__(self):
        # record the start time
        self.time_start = perf_counter()
        # return this object
        return self

    # exit the async context manager
    async def __aexit__(self, exc_type, exc, tb):
        # record the end time
        self.time_end = perf_counter()
        # calculate the duration
        self.duration = self.time_end - self.time_start
        # report the duration
        print(f'{self.name} took {self.duration:.3f} s')
        # do not suppress any exception
        return False

# task to benchmark
async def work():
    # create a large list
    data = [i*i for i in range(100000000)]

# main coroutine
async def main():
    # report a message
    print('Main starting')
    # create the task
    task = asyncio.create_task(work())
    # benchmark the execution of our task
    async with Benchmark('work()'):
        await task
    # report a message
    print('Main done')
```

```
# start the event loop
asyncio.run(main())
```

Running the example first starts the asyncio event loop and runs the `main()` coroutine.

The `main()` coroutine runs and reports a message. It then creates an `asyncio.Task` for our `work()` coroutine.

Next, the `main()` coroutine creates the Benchmark asynchronous context manager via the `async with` expression and provides the name `"work()"`, which is stored in an object attribute.

The `main()` coroutine suspends and the context manager is entered, automatically awaiting the `__aenter__()` coroutine where the start time is recorded in an object attribute.

Our task is then awaited in the body of the context manager. The `work()` task runs and the list is created.

Finally, the asynchronous context manager is exited, automatically awaiting the `__aexit__()` method, recording the end time, calculating the duration, and reporting it to standard out.

In this case, we can see that the `task()` coroutine took about 6.279 seconds to complete.

Note, the results on your system may differ.

This highlights how we can benchmark an arbitrary `asyncio.Task` using a custom asynchronous context manager.

```
Main starting
work() took 6.279 s
Main done
```

19.5   Further Reading

This section lists helpful additional resources on the topic.

- `asyncio` – Asynchronous I/O.
  https://docs.python.org/3/library/asyncio.html
- `time` – Time access and conversions.
  https://docs.python.org/3/library/time.html
- Python Data model.
  https://docs.python.org/3/reference/datamodel.html

19.6 Takeaways

You now know how to benchmark asyncio using an asynchronous context manager.

Specifically, you know:

- How to develop an asynchronous context manager to benchmark coroutines and tasks.
- How to use an asynchronous context manager for benchmarking in asyncio.

19.6.1 Next

In the next tutorial, we will explore how to develop a benchmark coroutine decorator.

Chapter 20

Benchmark Coroutine Decorator

You can develop a custom benchmark decorator that will automatically record and report the execution time of target coroutines in asyncio programs.

This requires defining the decorator and adding the decoration to the coroutine to be benchmarked.

In this tutorial, you will discover how to automatically benchmark target coroutines using a benchmark decorator in Python.

After completing this tutorial, you will know:

- How to use a coroutine decorator to benchmark target coroutines in asyncio.
- How to develop a custom function decorator that supports benchmarking coroutines instead of functions.
- How to develop a custom coroutine decorator that is robust to task cancellation.

Let's get started.

20.1 Need A Benchmark Coroutine Decorator

We have seen in a previous chapter how to develop a benchmark function decorator.

The decorator can be added to any arbitrary function and it will automatically record the start and end times, and then calculate and report the overall execution time.

The way the function decorator is implemented is that it calls a target function on the callers behalf.

The problem is, we cannot use this type of decorator to benchmark coroutines in asyncio programs.

The reason is that we do not call a coroutine, instead we construct and await it. Therefore attempting to benchmark coroutines using a function decorator results in an error.

Additionally, a coroutine can be canceled at any time. We may want to expect the cancellation and use it as an appropriate point to stop the benchmarking of the target coroutine.

As such, we need to develop a function decorator that is tailored for coroutines. We need to develop a benchmark coroutine decorator.

20.2 How To Develop A Benchmark Coroutine Decorator

We can develop our custom coroutine decorator to automatically benchmark our target coroutines.

This involves a few steps, they are:

1. How to create a coroutine decorator.
2. How to develop a coroutine that benchmarks a target coroutine.

Let's dive in.

20.2.1   Coroutine Decorators

We can develop a decorator for coroutines instead of functions.

This can be achieved by changing the inner function to a coroutine, e.g. defined using the **async def** expression.

Instead of calling a target function, the inner coroutine must await the target coroutine and pass along any arguments and return any return values.

For example:

```
# define the custom decorator
def custom_decorator(coro):
    # inner coroutine that wraps the target coroutine
    @wraps(coro)
    def inner_wrapper(*args, **kwargs):
        # await the target
        return await coro(*args, **kwargs)
```

To use the decorator on a target coroutine, we add it to the coroutine just like we did above for a target function.

For example:

```
@custom_decorator
async def work():
    # ...
```

Next, let's look at how we can define custom coroutine decorators to automatically benchmark our target coroutines.

20.2.2   Benchmark Coroutine Decorator

We can develop a coroutine decorator to benchmark a target coroutine automatically.

The decorator will be called **benchmark()** and take the name of the coroutine to be decorated as an argument.

```
# define the benchmark decorator
def benchmark(coro):
    # ...
```

Next, we can define the inner wrapper coroutine.

It must take arguments for the target coroutine, just in case they are needed. It then must record the start time before awaiting the target coroutine, and the end time after awaiting the target coroutine.

We will use the `time.perf_counter()` time function, preferred for benchmarking.

It then calculates the execution time and reports it before returning any return value from the target coroutine itself.

For example:

```
# inner coroutine that wraps the target coro
@wraps(coro)
async def wrapped(*args, **kwargs):
    # record start time
    time_start = perf_counter()
    # await the target
    return await coro(*args, **kwargs)
    # record end time
    time_end = perf_counter()
    # calculate the duration
    time_duration = time_end - time_start
    # report the duration
    name = coro.__name__
    print(f'{name} Took {time_duration:.3f} s')
```

One issue is that a coroutine may be canceled at any time.

As such, we may want to record and report the execution time of the target, even if it is canceled.

This can be achieved by wrapping the awaited target coroutine in a try-finally structure and recording and reporting the execution time in the finally block.

For example:

```python
# inner coroutine that wraps the target coro
@wraps(coro)
async def wrapped(*args, **kwargs):
    # record start time
    time_start = perf_counter()
    try:
        # await the target
        return await coro(*args, **kwargs)
    finally:
        # record end time
        time_end = perf_counter()
        # calculate the duration
        time_duration = time_end - time_start
        # report the duration
        name = coro.__name__
        print(f'{name} Took {time_duration:.3f} s')
```

This will ensure that even if the target coroutine is canceled, it will still report the execution time.

Tying this together, the complete decorator for benchmarking target coroutines is listed below.

```python
# define the benchmark decorator
def benchmark(coro):
    # inner coroutine that wraps the target coro
    @wraps(coro)
    async def wrapped(*args, **kwargs):
        # record start time
        time_start = perf_counter()
        try:
            # await the target
            return await coro(*args, **kwargs)
        finally:
            # record end time
            time_end = perf_counter()
            # calculate the duration
```

```
        time_duration = time_end - time_start
        # report the duration
        name = coro.__name__
        print(f'{name} Took {time_duration:.3f} s')
    # return the wrapped coro
    return wrapped
```

Finally, to use the decorator, we add @benchmark above the target coroutine.

For example:

```
@benchmark
async def custom_coroutine():
    # ...
```

Now that we know how to develop a benchmark coroutine decorator, let's look at a worked example.

20.3 Example Of Benchmarking A Coroutine

We can explore how to use our benchmark decorator to benchmark the execution time of a custom coroutine.

In this example, we will define a custom coroutine that takes a moment to complete.

The coroutine creates a list of 100 million squared integers in a list comprehension. This will block the asyncio event loop for the duration.

For example:

```
# work to benchmark
async def work():
    # create a large list
    data = [i*i for i in range(100000000)]
```

We can then add our **@benchmark** decoration to our **task()** coroutine.

```
# work to benchmark
@benchmark
async def work():
    # create a large list
    data = [i*i for i in range(100000000)]
```

Then, all we need to do is await our **work()** coroutine from the entry point of the program and it will be benchmarked automatically.

Tying this together, the complete example of using our coroutine decorator to estimate the duration of our **work()** target coroutine is listed below.

```
# SuperFastPython.com
# example of benchmarking a coroutine with a decorator
from time import perf_counter
from functools import wraps
import asyncio

# define the benchmark decorator
def benchmark(coro):
    # inner coroutine that wraps the target coro
    @wraps(coro)
    async def wrapped(*args, **kwargs):
        # record start time
        time_start = perf_counter()
        try:
            # await the target
            return await coro(*args, **kwargs)
        finally:
            # record end time
            time_end = perf_counter()
            # calculate the duration
            time_duration = time_end - time_start
            # report the duration
            name = coro.__name__
            print(f'{name} Took {time_duration:.3f} s')
```

```
    # return the wrapped coro
    return wrapped

# work to benchmark
@benchmark
async def work():
    # create a large list
    data = [i*i for i in range(100000000)]

# main coroutine
async def main():
    # report a message
    print('Main starting')
    # benchmark the execution of our task
    await work()
    # report a message
    print('Main done')

# start the event loop
asyncio.run(main())
```

Running the program starts the asyncio event loop and runs the main() coroutine.

The main() coroutine runs and reports an initial message before awaiting the work() coroutine.

The benchmark decorator runs and records the start time.

It then awaits the work() coroutine with any arguments provided, in this case, no arguments.

The work() coroutine runs and creates a list of 100 million squared integers before terminating.

The inner benchmark coroutine records the end time and then calculates the execution time. The execution time is then reported to standard output.

The inner benchmark coroutine terminates and the main() coroutine resumes and reports a final message before the program exits.

In this case, we can see that the `work()` coroutine took about 6.305 seconds to complete.

Note, the results on your system may differ.

This highlights how we can benchmark arbitrary coroutines using our benchmark decorator.

```
Main starting
work Took 6.305 seconds
Main done
```

20.4 Further Reading

This section lists helpful additional resources on the topic.

- `asyncio` – Asynchronous I/O.
  https://docs.python.org/3/library/asyncio.html
- `time` – Time access and conversions.
  https://docs.python.org/3/library/time.html
- `functools` – Higher-order functions and operations on callable objects.
  https://docs.python.org/3/library/functools.html

20.5 Takeaways

You now know how to automatically benchmark target coroutines using a benchmark decorator in Python.

Specifically, you know:

- How to use a coroutine decorator to benchmark target coroutines in asyncio.
- How to develop a custom function decorator that supports benchmarking coroutines instead of functions.
- How to develop a custom coroutine decorator that is robust to task cancellation.

20.5.1   Next

In the next tutorial, we will explore how to use the `timeit` module for benchmarking.

Part VI

Benchmarking With timeit

The `time` module provides a suite of tools for getting the time.

As we have seen, we can use the functions in the `time` module to benchmark Python code, but the module and the functions were not specifically developed for benchmarking.

The `timeit` module on the other hand was specifically developed for benchmarking.

It includes two interfaces: a programming and command line interface.

It also encodes best practices directly into the module, including repeated benchmarking and the use of high-precision timers.

The chapters that follow explore how we can benchmark our Python code using the `timeit` module.

Chapter 21

Benchmarking With The `timeit` Module

You can benchmark snippets of Python code using the `timeit` module in the standard library.

In this tutorial, you will discover how to benchmark Python code using the `timeit` module.

After completing this tutorial, you will know:

- What the `timeit` module is and the types of tasks to which it is suited.
- The best practices encoded into the `timeit` module.

Let's get started.

21.1   What Is `timeit`?

The `timeit` module is provided in the Python standard library.

It provides an easy way to benchmark single statements and snippets of Python code.

> This module provides a simple way to time small bits of Python code. It has both a Command-Line Interface as

well as a callable one. It avoids a number of common traps for measuring execution times.

– `timeit` – Measure execution time of small code snippets.

The `timeit` module allows us to answer code performance questions, such as:

1. How long does a particular function or code block take to run?
2. Which of two different code implementations is faster?
3. What is the execution time of specific lines of code within a larger program?

The primary goal of `timeit` is to provide accurate and repeatable timing measurements, helping us identify performance bottlenecks and evaluate the impact of code optimizations.

21.1.1 The `timeit` Module Has Two Interfaces

The `timeit` module provides two interfaces for benchmarking, they are:

1. API interface.
2. Command-line interface.

The first is an API that can be used via the `timeit.Timer` object or `timeit.timeit()` and `timeit.repeat()` module functions.

The second is a command line interface.

Both are intended to benchmark single statements, although multiple lines and multiple statements can be benchmarked using the module.

We will explore how to uses these two interfaces in the following chapters.

21.1.2 The `timeit` Module Encodes Best Practices

Importantly the `timeit` module it encodes a number of best practices for benchmarking, including:

- Timing code using `time.perf_counter()`, for high-precision.
- Executing target code many times by default (many samples), to reduce statistical noise.
- Disabling the Python garbage collector, to reduce the variance in the measurements.
- Providing a controlled and well-defined scope for benchmarked code, to reduce unwanted side-effects.

This means that we can focus on what code to benchmark and what the results mean, rather than focusing on how the benchmark is measured and reported.

> Note By default, `timeit()` temporarily turns off garbage collection during the timing. The advantage of this approach is that it makes independent timings more comparable.

– `timeit` – Measure execution time of small code snippets.

21.1.3 The `timeit` Module Is For Code Snippets

The `timeit` module is intended to benchmark small amounts of code that run very fast.

> Class for timing execution speed of small code snippets.

– `timeit` – Measure execution time of small code snippets.

It is generally not intended for benchmarking entire programs, although it can.

The interface is designed to take a single statement of code.

It is also generally not intended for benchmarking slow code, e.g. that takes seconds, minutes, or longer to run, although it can.

The benchmarking uses a high-precision timer that reports process time and executes a given statement many times by default to expose the runtime signal of very short-duration target code.

If larger sections of code need to be benchmarked or target code has a long duration, consider developing custom benchmarking code that makes use of `time.time()` or `time.perf_counter()`, or use the time Unix command.

Next, let's consider the mindset needed when using the `timeit` module.

21.2   What Is The `timeit` Mindset

Using the `timeit` module can be confusing to developers when used for the first time.

There are three main areas of confusion.

1. We must specify the scope required for the benchmark code.
2. Benchmark times are not wall-clock times.
3. Benchmarked code is executed many many times, e.g. thousands of times by default.

This is intentional, capturing benchmarking best practices, but requires a mindset shift.

21.2.1   Specify Scope

The code to be benchmarked must be specified as a string.

Additionally, the scope required to execute the benchmark code must be specified.

This can be achieved either via a setup string that might define or assign required variables or by specifying `globals` (global variables) that include the state and definitions required to execute the benchmark code.

This is required because the benchmarking of code is isolated from the program. This is intentional as it limits unwanted side effects of the program on the benchmark code, potentially influencing the benchmark score.

21.2.2 Benchmark Timings

The benchmarking scores reported are in a given unit of time appropriate for the execution time.

Times are reported using an internal performance timer, different from the system clock.

The reason is that system clock time can be unreliable across multiple platforms, as used by functions such as functions like `time.time()`.

Instead, a standardized high-performance timer is used by default via the `time.perf_counter()` function.

> Return the value (in fractional seconds) of a performance counter, i.e. a clock with the highest available resolution to measure a short duration. It does include time elapsed during sleep and is system-wide.

– time – Time access and conversions.

Additionally, scores are a summary statistic, such as the sum or minimum of multiple benchmark runs.

This means that benchmark times can be compared relatively, but not used to define absolute execution times.

21.2.3 Repeated Benchmarks

Each benchmark is repeated many times by default, e.g. thousands times.

The reason is that executing a single statement may take a very small interval of time. This is both hard to measure and also strongly influenced by whatever else might be happening on the system at the same time.

Executing the benchmark code many times allows the execution time signal to rise and overwhelm any statistical noise and variance.

As long as other benchmark statements use the same number of repetitions, the resulting numbers can be compared relatively, but they cannot be used as absolute benchmark scores.

Next, let's explore how we might use the `timeit` API.

21.3   Further Reading

This section lists helpful additional resources on the topic.

- `time` – Time access and conversions.
  https://docs.python.org/3/library/time.html
- `timeit` – Measure execution time of small code snippets.
  https://docs.python.org/3/library/timeit.html

21.4   Takeaways

You now know how to benchmark Python code using the `timeit` module.

Specifically, you know:

- What the `timeit` module is and the types of tasks to which it is suited.
- The best practices encoded into the `timeit` module.

21.4.1   Next

In the next tutorial, we will explore how to benchmark using the `timeit` module API.

Chapter 22

Benchmarking With `timeit.timeit()`

You can benchmark snippets of Python code using the `timeit.timeit()` function.

In this tutorial, you will discover how to benchmark Python code using the `timeit.timeit()` function.

After completing this tutorial, you will know:

- How to use and customize the configuration of the `timeit.timeit()` function for benchmarking.
- How to benchmark standalone code and code that requires setup with the `timeit.timeit()` function.
- How to benchmark custom functions using the `timeit.timeit()` function.

Let's get started.

22.1   Overview Of The `timeit` API

The focus of the `timeit` API is the `timeit.Timer` class, which can be used simply via the `timeit.timeit()` and `timeit.repeat()` module functions.

This tutorial will focus on how to use the `timeit.timeit()` function, the recommended approach.

Nevertheless, before we dive into the `timeit.timeit()` function, let's take a moment to review the `timeit.Timer` class and `timeit.repeat()` module function.

22.1.1 How To Use Timer()

The `timeit.Timer` class can be used by first creating an instance and then either calling the `timeit()` or `repeat()` methods.

Class for timing execution speed of small code snippets.

– `timeit` – Measure execution time of small code snippets.

The `timeit.Timer` class constructor takes the details of the code that is being benchmarked, including the statement, any **setup** and any **globals** namespace.

For example:

```
...
# create a timer
timer = timeit.Timer('[i*i for i in range(1000)]')
```

The code can be benchmarked using the `timeit()` method that takes the number of times the code is run, which defaults to 1,000,000.

For example:

```
...
# benchmark a python statement
result = timer.timeit(number=100)
```

The code can be repeatedly benchmarked by calling the **repeat()** method.

This method takes a **repeat** argument that specifies the number of repetitions, defaulting to 5. It also takes a **number** argument specifying the number of times the code is run each repetition.

For example:

```
...
# benchmark a python statement repeatedly
results = timer.repeat(repeat=3, number=100)
```

The `Timer` class also provides an `autorange()` that will call `timeit()` and automatically determine the number of times to run the code to ensure the overall duration is large enough to be meaningful.

> This is a convenience function that calls `timeit()` repeatedly so that the total time $>= 0.2$ second, returning the eventual (number of loops, time taken for that number of loops). It calls `timeit()` with increasing numbers from the sequence 1, 2, 5, 10, 20, 50, ... until the time taken is at least 0.2 second.

– `timeit` – Measure execution time of small code snippets.

22.1.2 How To Use `repeat()`

The `timeit.repeat()` function will call the `timeit.timeit()` function many times, e.g. repeatedly.

> This is a convenience function that calls the `timeit()` repeatedly, returning a list of results.

– `timeit` – Measure execution time of small code snippets.

It returns a collection of benchmark results that can then be summarized, such as the minimum (fastest time).

The average (expected time) or the maximum (longest time) can be reported, but are not likely to be representative, as many factors can cause a benchmark to take longer than expected.

> Note: It's tempting to calculate mean and standard deviation from the result vector and report these. However, this is not very useful. In a typical case, the lowest value gives a lower bound for how fast your machine can run the given code snippet; higher values in the result vector are typically not caused by variability in Python's speed, but

by other processes interfering with your timing accuracy.
So the `min()` of the result is probably the only number
you should be interested in. After that, you should look
at the entire vector and apply common sense rather than
statistics.

– `timeit` – Measure execution time of small code snippets.

Like the `timeit.timeit()` function, the `timeit.repeat()` function
takes the statement to be benchmarked, along with a `setup`, `number`,
and `globals` arguments.

For example:

```
...
# benchmark a python statement repeatedly
results = timeit.repeat('[i*i for i in range(1000)]')
```

The number of repetitions is specified via the `repeat` argument which
is set to 5 by default.

For example:

```
...
# benchmark a python statement repeatedly
results = timeit.repeat(
    '[i*i for i in range(1000)]', repeat=10)
```

Now that we have had a look at the `timeit.Timer` class and
`timeit.repeat()` module function, let's take a closer look at the
`timeit.timeit()` function.

22.2   How To Benchmark With `timeit()`

The `timeit.timeit()` function benchmarks Python code and reports
the duration in seconds.

Create a Timer instance with the given statement, setup
code and timer function and run its `timeit()` method
with number executions.

– `timeit` – Measure execution time of small code snippets.

The `timeit.timeit()` function takes the Python statement to be benchmarked as a string.

For example:

```
...
# benchmark a python statement
result = timeit.timeit('[i*i for i in range(1000)]')
```

22.2.1   Setup Argument

Any code required to execute the target benchmark code can be provided as a string to the **setup** argument.

This might include defining a variable.

The setup code is only executed once prior to the benchmark.

For example:

```
...
# benchmark a python statement with setup code
result = timeit.timeit('[i*i for i in range(total)]',
    setup='total=10000')
```

It might include importing the main module so that required functions are imported.

For example:

```
...
# benchmark a python statement with import in setup
result = timeit.timeit('task()',
    setup='from __main__ import task')
```

22.2.2   Globals Argument

Alternatively, if we have defined code in our program that is required to execute the benchmark code, we can specify the **globals** argument to provide the entire namespace.

We can specify **locals()** or **globals()** which will include a namespace from our current program.

For example:
```
...
# benchmark a python statement with a namespace
result = timeit.timeit('task()', globals=globals())
```

22.2.3   Number Argument

Finally, we can specify the number of repetitions of the benchmark code via the **number** argument.

By default, this is set to one million, although can be set to a smaller number if the benchmark code takes a long time to execute.

For example:
```
...
# benchmark a python statement with a smaller number
result = timeit.timeit('[i*i for i in range(1000)]',
    number=100)
```

The **number** argument should be set so that the overall duration is at least 0.2 or 0.5 seconds, perhaps even more than one second.

Now that we know to use the `timeit.timeit()` module function, let's consider some tips and recommendations.

22.3   Benchmarking Recommendations

This section provides some recommendations when working with the `timeit.timeit()` module function.

22.3.1   Import __main__ Module

We can benchmark a function defined in our Python file.

This can be achieved by importing it from the main module in the **setup** argument, and making it available to the benchmark code.

For example:

```
...
# benchmark a function defined in main
result = timeit.timeit('task()',
    setup='from __main__ import task')
```

22.3.2 Pass globals()

We can benchmark code that requires data or functions defined in our program.

This can be achieved by specifying the namespace via the `globals` argument, such as either `locals()` for the current local namespace or `globals()` for the current global namespace.

This will make the relevant scope available to the benchmark code, including any defined variables and functions.

For example:

```
...
# benchmark custom functions
result = timeit.timeit('task()', globals=globals())
```

22.3.3 Benchmark Multiple Expressions

Although the `timeit` module is intended to benchmark single statements, we can use it to benchmark large snippets composed of multiple statements.

This can be achieved by creating a compound statement on one line, separated by semicolons (`;`).

For example:

```
...
# benchmark multiple statements
timeit.timeit(
    '[i*i for i in range(10)];[i+i for i in range(10)]')
```

Another approach is to put the target code into a function and benchmark a call to the function.

For example:

```
# function that defines a task
def task():
    [i*i for i in range(1000)]

# benchmark custom functions
result = timeit.timeit('task()', globals=globals())
```

Another approach is to define a multi-line statement as a multi-line string, then provide the string as an argument.

Now that we know how to get the most out of the `timeit.timeit()` function, let's look at some worked examples.

22.4   Example Of Benchmarking Standalone Code

In this example, we will benchmark standalone code.

This is code that does not depend on any other variables or functions.

We will benchmark two different ways to calculate a list of 1,000 squared numbers.

The first approach will multiply each number by itself.

```
[i*i for i in range(1000)]
```

The second approach will use the exponent operator (**) and raise each number to the power of 2.

```
[i**2 for i in range(1000)]
```

These snippets execute very quickly, therefore we will repeat each snippet 100,000 times when calling the `timeit.timeit()` function.

```
...
# benchmark the i*i method
time_method1 = timeit('[i*i for i in range(1000)]',
    number=100000)
```

```
...
# benchmark the i**2 method
time_method2 = timeit('[i**2 for i in range(1000)]',
    number=100000)
```

Tying this together, the complete example is listed below.

```
# SuperFastPython.com
# example of benchmarking list of numbers with timeit()
from timeit import timeit
# benchmark the i*i method
time_method1 = timeit('[i*i for i in range(1000)]',
    number=100000)
# report the duration
print(f'i*i: {time_method1:.3f} seconds')
# benchmark the i**2 method
time_method2 = timeit('[i**2 for i in range(1000)]',
    number=100000)
# report the duration
print(f'i**2: {time_method2:.3f} seconds')
```

Running the example first executes the `i*i` approach 100,000 times and reports the overall duration.

It then runs the `i**2` approach 100,000 times and reports the overall duration.

In this case, we can see that the `i*i` approach took about 4.186 seconds, whereas the `i**2` approach took about 5.535 seconds.

This suggests that the `i*i` approach is faster.

Note, the results on your system may differ.

This highlights how we can benchmark standalone code using `timeit.timeit()`.

```
i*i: 4.186 seconds
i**2: 5.535 seconds
```

Next, let's look at including a benchmark that requires setup.

22.5   Example Of Benchmarking Code With Setup

We can explore a `timeit.timeit()` benchmark that requires setup code.

In this case, we will add one more approach to the benchmark suite for squaring a list of 1,000 numbers.

The new approach will use the `math.pow()` function, which takes the number and the exponent as arguments.

```
pow(i,2) for i in range(1000)
```

This requires that the `pow()` function be imported from the math module.

We can achieve this by including the important statement via the `setup` argument to the `timeit.timeit()` function.

```
...
# benchmark the math.pow() method
time_method3 = timeit('[pow(i,2) for i in range(1000)]',
    setup='from math import pow', number=100000)
```

Tying this together, the complete example is listed below.

```
# SuperFastPython.com
# example of benchmarking list of numbers with timeit()
from timeit import timeit
# benchmark the i*i method
time_method1 = timeit('[i*i for i in range(1000)]',
    number=100000)
# report the duration
print(f'i*i: {time_method1:.3f} seconds')
# benchmark the i**2 method
time_method2 = timeit('[i**2 for i in range(1000)]',
    number=100000)
# report the duration
print(f'i**2: {time_method2:.3f} seconds')
```

```
# benchmark the math.pow() method
time_method3 = timeit('[pow(i,2) for i in range(1000)]',
    setup='from math import pow', number=100000)
# report the duration
print(f'math.pow(): {time_method3:.3f} seconds')
```

In this case, we benchmark the `i*i` and `i**2` approaches as before, achieving similar but not identical results, specifically, 4.229 seconds and 5.412 seconds respectively.

Then the new **math.pow()** approach is benchmarked. In this case, it takes about 9.223 seconds to complete overall.

We can see that it is more than twice as slow as the `i*i` approach.

Note, the results on your system may differ.

This highlights how we can benchmark a function that requires importing using `timeit.timeit()`.

```
i*i: 4.229 seconds
i**2: 5.412 seconds
math.pow(): 9.223 seconds
```

Next, we will explore how we can benchmark a custom function.

22.6 Example Of Benchmarking A Custom Function

We can explore a `timeit.timeit()` benchmark of a custom function.

In this case, we will define a new function that squares a given number.

```
# define a custom function for squaring numbers
def square(value):
    return value * value
```

We will then create a list of 1,000 squared integers that use our custom function.

```
[square(i) for i in range(1000)]
```

This requires that the **square()** function be made available to the benchmark snippet.

We can achieve this via the **globals** argument and provide the current namespace via the **globals()** built-in function, which will include the definition of our custom **square()** function.

```
...
# benchmark the square() method
time_method4 = timeit('[square(i) for i in range(1000)]',
    globals=globals(), number=100000)
```

Tying this together, the complete example is listed below.

```
# SuperFastPython.com
# example of benchmarking list of numbers with timeit()
from timeit import timeit

# define a custom function for squaring numbers
def square(value):
    return value * value

# benchmark the i*i method
time_method1 = timeit('[i*i for i in range(1000)]',
    number=100000)
# report the duration
print(f'i*i: {time_method1:.3f} seconds')
# benchmark the i**2 method
time_method2 = timeit('[i**2 for i in range(1000)]',
    number=100000)
# report the duration
print(f'i**2: {time_method2:.3f} seconds')
# benchmark the math.pow() method
time_method3 = timeit('[pow(i,2) for i in range(1000)]',
    setup='from math import pow', number=100000)
# report the duration
print(f'math.pow(): {time_method3:.3f} seconds')
```

```
# benchmark the square() method
time_method4 = timeit(
    '[square(i) for i in range(1000)]',
    globals=globals(), number=100000)
# report the duration
print(f'square(): {time_method4:.3f} seconds')
```

In this case, we benchmark the i*i, i**2, and math.pow() approaches as before, achieving similar but not identical results, specifically, 4.222 seconds, 5.551 seconds, and 9.237 seconds respectively.

Then the new custom square() function approach is benchmarked. In this case, it completes in about 7.231 seconds.

This is slower than the simple i*i approach, although it is faster than the math.pow() approach.

Note, the results on your system may differ.

This highlights how we can benchmark a custom function using timeit.timeit().

```
i*i: 4.222 seconds
i**2: 5.551 seconds
math.pow(): 9.237 seconds
square(): 7.231 seconds
```

22.7 Further Reading

This section lists helpful additional resources on the topic.

- timeit – Measure execution time of small code snippets.
  https://docs.python.org/3/library/timeit.html
- math – Mathematical functions.
  https://docs.python.org/3/library/math.html

22.8   Takeaways

You now know how to benchmark Python code using the `timeit.timeit()` function.

Specifically, you know:

- How to use and customize the configuration of the `timeit.timeit()` function for benchmarking.
- How to benchmark standalone code and code that requires setup with the `timeit.timeit()` function.
- How to benchmark custom functions using the `timeit.timeit()` function.

22.8.1   Next

In the next tutorial, we will explore how to benchmark using the `timeit` module command line interface.

Chapter 23

Benchmarking With The `timeit` Command Line

You can benchmark snippets of Python code on the command line by using the `timeit` module.

In this tutorial, you will discover how to use the `timeit` command line interface to benchmark code in Python.

After completing this tutorial, you will know:

- What is the command line interface and how to execute Python code and modules from the command line.
- How to use the `timeit` module for benchmarking code snippets from the command line.
- How to customize the benchmarking of code snippets using the `timeit` from the command line interface.

Let's get started.

23.1 What Is A Command Line Interface

The command line or command line interface is a way of interacting with the computer using text commands, as opposed to clicking around on a graphical interface with a mouse.

> A command-line interface (CLI) is a means of interacting with a device or computer program with commands from a user or client, and responses from the device or program, in the form of lines of text.

– Command-line interface, Wikipedia.

It is known by different names on different platforms, typically after the name of the program that provides the interface.

For example: "Command Prompt" in Windows, "Terminal" in macOS, and "Shell" in Unix.

Python can be used on the command line directly via the `python` command.

This will open the Python interpreter.

We can also call the Python interpreter with flags. For example, we can execute a line of code directly using the Python interpreter via the -c flag:

```
python -c "print('hello world')"
```

This will start the Python interpreter, execute the line of code, report the result, and close the interpreter.

Now that we know about the command line, let's look at the command line interface for the `timeit` module.

23.2 How To Use The `timeit` Command Line Interface

A Python module can be run as a command on the command line directly via the -m flag, followed by the module name.

```
-m mod : run library module as a script
```

The `timeit` module can be run directly in this way, for example:

```
python -m timeit [-n N] [-r N] [-u U] [-s S] [-h] [...]
```

The flags must always come first, and the statement that is being benchmarked must always come last, otherwise, we will get an error.

The main command line flags (or switches) to the `timeit` module are as follows:

- -n N or --number=N: how many times to execute "statement"
- -r N or --repeat=N: how many times to repeat the timer (default 5)
- -s S or --setup=S: statement to be executed once initially (default pass)
- -u U or --unit=U: the units for the result, e.g. nsec, usec, msec, or sec.

Other flags are provided, such as the -p or --process flag to change the way that time is measured, -v or --verbose flag for verbose output, and the -h or --help flag for getting a list of all available flags.

If the -n flag is not provided, the `timeit` module will attempt to estimate the number of times to run the statement until a minimum time threshold is reached.

> If -n is not given, a suitable number of loops is calculated by trying increasing numbers from the sequence 1, 2, 5, 10, 20, 50, ... until the total time is at least 0.2 seconds.

– `timeit` – Measure execution time of small code snippets.

The units for the -u flag can be confusing, below a guide:

- **nsec**: Nanoseconds (1000 nanoseconds = 1 microsecond)
- **usec**: Microseconds (1000 microsecond = 1 milliseconds)
- **msec**: Milliseconds (1000 milliseconds = 1 second)
- **sec**: Seconds (60 seconds = 1 minute)

The result is a benchmark result with the format:

```
[n] loops, best of [r]: [time] [units] per loop
```

Where:

- **[n]** is the number of times the statement was executed.
- **[r]** is the number of repeats of **n** loops.
- **[time]** average time to execute the statement from the fastest repetition.
- **[units]** is the time units in which the result is reported.

This means if the statement is executed 1,000 times and is repeated 5 times then the statement is executed 5,000 times and the fastest time from the 5 repetitions is reported.

The reported time is an average from the best repetition:

- $\text{time} = \frac{\text{duration of fastest repetition}}{\text{number of executions}}$

This means that the one repetition of 5 that was the fastest (best) was used and the total time of all runs was divided by the number of runs, which was 5,000, to give the expected or average runtime for the statement.

> In the output, there are three fields. The loop count, which tells you how many times the statement body was run per timing loop repetition. The repetition count ('best of 5') which tells you how many times the timing loop was repeated, and finally the time the statement body took on average within the best repetition of the timing loop. That is, the time the fastest repetition took divided by the loop count.

– `timeit` – Measure execution time of small code snippets.

The `timeit` command line interface cannot benchmark a Python program directly.

Instead, it is intended to benchmark statements that execute in a short duration of time.

Now that we know the basics of the `timeit` command line interface, let's look at some worked examples.

23.3 Example Of Benchmarking Standalone Code

We can explore how to benchmark a standalone code snippet using the `timeit` command line interface.

In this case, we will benchmark a snippet that creates a list of 1,000 squared integers.

```
[i*i for i in range(1000)]
```

For example:

```
python -m timeit "[i*i for i in range(1000)]"
```

Running this command on the command line, we see output from the `timeit` module.

In this case, we can see that the statement was executed 10,000 times and this loop was repeated 5 times, so 50,000 runs of the code.

The estimated time was `40.8 usec`, where `usec` is a microsecond. This means on the fastest or best repetition the statement took about 40.8 microseconds on average to run.

Note, the results on your system may differ.

```
10000 loops, best of 5: 40.8 usec per loop
```

Let's try another standalone version of creating a list of squared numbers.

In this case, using the ** operator.

```
[i**2 for i in range(1000)]
```

We can benchmark this on the command line with `timeit` as follows:

```
python -m timeit "[i**2 for i in range(1000)]"
```

Running this command on the command line, we see output from the `timeit` module.

In this case, we can see that the statement was executed 5,000 times and this was repeated 5 times. This means that the statement was executed 25,000 times.

The estimated time was about `53.8 usec`, that is the average run time for the statement, or the best repetition was about 53.8 microseconds.

Note, the results on your system may differ.

This highlights how we can use the `timeit` command line interface to benchmark standalone code.

```
5000 loops, best of 5: 53.8 usec per loop
```

Notice that the `timeit` module automatically chose the number of loops, differing between each benchmark. This may be a problem if we want a fair apples-to-apples comparison.

23.4   Example Of Benchmarking With Custom Loops

A problem with the previous example is that the number of loop iterations of the statement differed across different statements being benchmarked.

We can fix the number of repetitions to ensure that we have an apples-to-apples comparison.

This can be achieved via the -n flag, which we can set to 10,000, chosen arbitrarily.

We can then benchmark the first statement again with a fixed number of iterations.

```
python -m timeit -n 10000 "[i*i for i in range(1000)]"
```

Running this command on the command line, we see output from the `timeit` module.

In this case, we can see that the number of repetitions is fixed at 10,000 as we expect and the average time from the best repetition was about 40.9 microseconds on average.

Note, the results on your system may differ.

```
10000 loops, best of 5: 40.9 usec per loop
```

We can also repeat the benchmark of the ** approach with a fixed number of loop iterations.

```
python -m timeit -n 10000 "[i**2 for i in range(1000)]"
```

Running this command on the command line, we see output from the `timeit` module.

In this case, we can see that the number of loop iterations is again fixed at 10,000 as we expect, and that the average time to execute the statement in the best repetition was about 53.8 microseconds on average.

Note, the results on your system may differ.

This highlights how we can use the `timeit` command line interface to benchmark code with a custom number of iterations per loop.

```
10000 loops, best of 5: 53.8 usec per loop
```

One limitation of these results is that few people understand what microseconds are.

23.5   Example Of Benchmarking With Custom Units

We can benchmark a statement with `timeit` and specify custom time units of measure.

Most people are familiar with seconds, so we can change the units from the default to seconds.

This can be achieved via the `-u` flag and providing the string `sec`.

We can then re-benchmark our squared list example.

```
python -m timeit -u sec "[i*i for i in range(1000)]"
```

Running this command on the command line, we see output from the `timeit` module.

In this case, we can see that the result is reported in seconds, but it is squashed and presented using scientific notation.

We can convert it back to decimal notation as follows:

- decimal = 4.11e-05
- decimal = 4.11×10^{-5}
- decimal = 4.11×0.00001
- decimal = 4.11×0.00001
- decimal = 0.0000411

Converted to decimal, the result is 0.0000411 seconds.

We can see why `timeit` automatically chose microseconds units to report the results above.

Note, the results on your system may differ.

This highlights how we can use the `timeit` command line interface to benchmark code with custom time units.

```
5000 loops, best of 5: 4.11e-05 sec per loop
```

23.6   Example Of Benchmarking With Custom Repetitions

Repeating a benchmark allows us to control for statistical noise.

Each tie we run a benchmark we will get a slightly different result. This is because of small differences in what the underlying operating system is doing at the same time as running the benchmark.

Repeating the benchmark many times means we can control for these background effects and choose the run with the minimum time, to give a fair idea of what is possible. From that run the average time to execute the statement is returned.

We can increase the number of repetitions of the benchmark loop in order to control more for the natural variation in the results. Increasing the number of repetitions from 5 to 10 or 30, or even 100 can help to ensure the results are more consistent from run to run.

This can be achieved via the **-r** flag. In this case, we will increase it to 100.

We can then re-benchmark our list of squared numbers examples.

```
python -m timeit -r 100 "[i*i for i in range(1000)]"
```

Running this command on the command line, we see output from the `timeit` module.

In this case, the average time to execute the statement was about 40.2 microseconds.

Note, the results on your system may differ.

```
5000 loops, best of 100: 40.4 usec per loop
```

Next, let's repeat the same test again and see if we get much variance in the result.

```
python -m timeit -r 100 "[i*i for i in range(1000)]"
```

Running this command on the command line, we see output from the `timeit` module.

Again we see the same result of about 40.4 microseconds.

Note, the results on your system may differ.

```
5000 loops, best of 100: 40.4 usec per loop
```

Now, we can decrease the number of repetitions to 3 and we should see a greater variance between two runs of the same benchmark.

```
python -m timeit -r 3 "[i*i for i in range(1000)]"
```

The first run gives an average time of 40.7 microseconds.

```
5000 loops, best of 3: 40.7 usec per loop
```

```
python -m timeit -r 3 "[i*i for i in range(1000)]"
```

The second run gives an average time of 40.8 microseconds.

Note, the results on your system may differ.

```
5000 loops, best of 3: 40.8 usec per loop
```

At least in this case, we see that increasing repetitions of the test has the effect of producing more stable and consistent results across independent benchmarks on the same machine.

23.7   Example Of Benchmarking With Verbose Output

By default, the `timeit` command line interface will repeat the looped execution of the provided statement 5 times.

We can see the total duration of each of these repetitions using the -v verbose flag.

We can apply this to our benchmark of calculating a list of squared numbers.

```
python -m timeit -v "[i*i for i in range(1000)]"
```

Running this command on the command line, we see output from the `timeit` module.

We did not specify the number of loops, therefore the `timeit` module automatically increased the number of loop iterations until the overall duration of one repetition was above 0.2 seconds.

We can see that it automatically chooses 5,000 iterations per loop and repeats the loop 5 times.

We can see the total times for each repetition, with a fast raw time of about 204 milliseconds.

If we divide this by the number of iterations, 5,000, this gives 0.0408 milliseconds. Converted to microseconds by multiplying 0.0408 by 1,000, this gives about 40.8 microseconds that we see reported at the bottom of the output.

Note, the results on your system may differ.

This highlights how we can use the `timeit` command line interface to benchmark code with verbose output.

```
1 loop -> 5.36e-05 secs
2 loops -> 8.32e-05 secs
5 loops -> 0.000205 secs
10 loops -> 0.000407 secs
20 loops -> 0.000843 secs
50 loops -> 0.00211 secs
100 loops -> 0.00405 secs
200 loops -> 0.00822 secs
500 loops -> 0.0207 secs
1000 loops -> 0.0413 secs
2000 loops -> 0.0814 secs
5000 loops -> 0.202 secs

raw times: 204 msec, 207 msec, 207 msec, 208 msec, ...
```

```
5000 loops, best of 5: 40.8 usec per loop
```

23.8 Example Of Benchmarking With Setup

We can benchmark statements that require some setup, such as importing a function.

This can be achieved via the -s flag and specifying the setup statement or statements.

We can explore an alternate way to calculate a list of squared numbers using the **math.pow()** function.

This requires that we import the **pow()** function from the math module.

For example:

```
-s "from math import pow"
```

We can benchmark this method using **timeit** as follows:

```
python -m timeit -s "from math import pow" \
    "[pow(i,2) for i in range(1000)]"
```

Running this command on the command line, we see output from the **timeit** module.

We can see that the statement was executed 5,000 times automatically with 5 loops. The average time from the best repetition was 92.6 microseconds.

Note, the results on your system may differ.

This highlights how we can use the **timeit** command line interface to benchmark code that requires setup.

```
5000 loops, best of 5: 92.6 usec per loop
```

23.9 Example Of Benchmarking With A Custom Function

We can use the `timeit` command line interface to benchmark a custom function.

Firstly, the custom function must be saved to a Python file. It can then be imported via the -s setup flag.

In this example, we will define a custom function for calculating squared numbers called `square()`.

```
# define a custom function for squaring numbers
def square(value):
    return value * value
```

We will save this in the current directly with the filename `square.py`

The `square()` function could then be imported into Python.

We can add this import statement to the setup of our `timeit` benchmark, for example:

```
-s "from square import square"
```

And then call the `square()` function when creating our list of 1,000 numbers

```
"[square(i) for i in range(1000)]"
```

Tying this together, the complete example of benchmarking a custom function is listed below.

```
python -m timeit -s "from square import square" \
    "[square(i) for i in range(1000)]"
```

Running this command on the command line, we see output from the `timeit` module.

In this case, we can see that `timeit` automatically chooses 5,000 loop iterations per repetition. The average time to execute the statement to construct the list with the custom function was 70.5 microseconds.

Note, the results on your system may differ.

This highlights how we can use the `timeit` command line interface to benchmark a custom function.

```
5000 loops, best of 5: 70.5 usec per loop
```

23.10   Example Of Getting Help

It is easy to forget the flags for the `timeit` module on the command line.

We can get help by using the -h flag.

For example:

```
python -m timeit -h
```

This reports a ton of helpful usage information for the `timeit` command line interface, including all of the command line flags and their purpose.

The output is omitted here for brevity.

23.11   Further Reading

This section lists helpful additional resources on the topic.

- Command-line interface, Wikipedia.
  https://en.wikipedia.org/wiki/Command-line_interface
- Scientific notation, Wikipedia.
  https://en.wikipedia.org/wiki/Scientific_notation
- `timeit` – Measure execution time of small code snippets.
  https://docs.python.org/3/library/timeit.html
- `math` – Mathematical functions.
  https://docs.python.org/3/library/math.html

23.12   Takeaways

You now know how to use the `timeit` command line interface to benchmark code in Python.

Specifically, you know:

- What is the command line interface and how to execute Python code and modules from the command line.
- How to use the `timeit` module for benchmarking code snippets from the command line.
- How to customize the benchmarking of code snippets using the `timeit` from the command line interface.

23.12.1   Next

In the next tutorial, we will explore other tools that are helpful when benchmarking.

Part VII

Other Benchmarking

The chapters in this part of the book explore other approaches we can use for benchmarking.

This includes command line tools available on most platforms, such as the `time` command, also called the `time` Unix command.

We also explore profiling via the `cProfile` and `profile` modules in the Python standard library.

Profiling is not the same as benchmarking, but is a related task that we can use to help discover the cause why code is slow so that we can change it. It is an activity we can perform while benchmarking, producing changes to code that can be benchmarked and compared to baseline versions of code.

The following chapters explore these alternate ways of benchmarking and related topics.

Chapter 24

Profile Python Code

You can profile slow Python programs to discover functions that occupy most of the runtime and functions that are called disproportionately more than any other.

The profilers built into the Python standard library are helpful in quickly discovering why some Python programs are slow and where to focus program optimization efforts.

In this tutorial, you will discover how to profile Python programs in order to discover why they are slow.

After completing this tutorial, you will know:

- What is code profiling and why it is important.
- How profiling is not benchmarking but an important and related task when optimizing performance.
- How to use the profiler in the standard library to find slow parts of Python code.

Let's get started.

24.1   What Is Code Profiling

Code profiling is a systematic and analytical technique used in software development to evaluate the runtime behavior of a program.

Its primary objective is to identify performance bottlenecks, memory inefficiencies, and other areas for improvement within the code.

Profiling provides valuable insights into how a program executes, allowing us to optimize it for better speed, efficiency, and resource utilization.

Profiling tools gather data on various aspects of program execution, including:

1. **CPU Usage**: Profilers monitor how much time the CPU spends on each function or method within the code. This information helps pinpoint functions that consume excessive CPU resources.
2. **Memory Usage**: They track memory allocations, deallocations, and usage patterns to identify memory leaks and inefficient memory management.
3. **Function Call Times**: Profilers record the time taken by each function or method, enabling us to focus on optimizing the most time-consuming parts of the code.
4. **I/O Operations**: Profilers can track input and output operations, helping us to optimize file, network, or database interactions.
5. **Call Graphs**: Profiling tools generate call graphs that illustrate the flow of function calls, making it clear which functions are called by others and their associated execution times.

By analyzing the data provided by profilers, we can make informed decisions about where to focus optimization efforts.

This might involve rewriting inefficient code, eliminating unnecessary function calls, reducing memory usage, or improving algorithmic efficiency.

Ultimately, profiling is an essential step in the software development process, ensuring that applications perform efficiently, use resources judiciously, and deliver a better user experience.

24.1.1 Need To Profile Slow Python Programs

Sometimes our Python programs are slow.

We can use profiling to help identify which parts of a Python program are slow so that we can change or fix them to be different or faster.

> In software engineering, profiling ("program profiling", "software profiling") is a form of dynamic program analysis that measures, for example, the space (memory) or time complexity of a program, the usage of particular instructions, or the frequency and duration of function calls. Most commonly, profiling information serves to aid program optimization, and more specifically, performance engineering.

– Profiling (computer programming), Wikipedia.

Profiling Python code is a valuable practice that offers several benefits.

Below are 5 of the best reasons we should profile our Python code:

1. **Performance Optimization**: Profiling helps identify performance bottlenecks and resource-intensive parts of your code. By pinpointing these areas, we can focus our optimization efforts to make our code faster and more efficient.
2. **Resource Management**: Profiling provides insights into how our code utilizes system resources such as CPU, memory, and I/O. This information is crucial for efficient resource management, preventing memory leaks, and ensuring optimal resource allocation.
3. **Prioritizing Improvements**: Profiling data helps us prioritize which parts of our codebase to optimize. Instead of making blind optimizations, we can concentrate our efforts where they will have the most significant impact.

4. **Reducing Overhead**: Profiling reveals unnecessary function calls, redundant operations, or inefficient algorithms. By addressing these issues, we can reduce computational overhead, leading to faster and more responsive applications.
5. **Enhancing User Experience**: In web applications or other software with user interfaces, profiling can lead to a better user experience. By optimizing code, we can reduce loading times, prevent lag, and provide a smoother and more responsive interaction for users.

Profiling is an essential tool in the software development toolkit, helping us to build more efficient and high-performing applications while optimizing resource usage.

Next, let's consider profiling as it relates to benchmarking.

24.1.2   Profiling Is Not Benchmarking

It is common to confuse profiling with benchmarking.

In fact, profiling code is a very different activity from benchmarking Python code.

They are two distinct techniques used in software development to assess and optimize performance, each with its unique goals and methodologies.

Benchmarking is primarily concerned with measuring the time it takes for a specific piece of code or an entire application to complete a given task. Its primary objective is to quantify the speed and efficiency of code execution.

Benchmarking provides answers to questions like:

- How long does this function take to run?
- How many operations can this code perform in a second?
- What is the response time of this application under a specific workload?

Importantly, benchmarking is commonly used to compare different implementations, versions, or configurations of code, assisting in the selection of the most efficient solution for a given task.

Profiling, in contrast, is focused on understanding how code behaves internally. It seeks to identify which parts of the code consume the most resources, such as CPU time, memory, or I/O operations.

Profiling dives into the nitty-gritty details of code execution, answering questions like:

- Which part of this program is the slowest?
- Which functions or methods are consuming the most CPU time?
- Where is memory being allocated and deallocated?

Profiling tools provide data at a fine-grained level, revealing specifics like function call counts, time spent in specific functions, and memory usage.

Profiling is an invaluable diagnostic tool used to uncover bottlenecks and pinpoint areas in the code that require optimization.

We can use profiling after benchmarking to identify areas of code that may be changed that are expected to reduce the overall execution time of the program.

Now that we know about profiling, let's look at how we can use the built-in Python profiler to do so.

24.2   How To Use The Python Profiler

Python provides an efficient C-based profiler in the `cProfile` module, built into the Python standard library.

A pure-Python profiler is provided in the `profile` module that offers the same API as the `cProfile` module. This can be used on those platforms that do not support the `cProfile` module.

> `cProfile` and `profile` provide deterministic profiling of Python programs. A profile is a set of statistics that describes how often and for how long various parts of the program executed.

– The Python Profilers

We can use the Python profiler via the command line interface.

You may recall that we can run a module as a Program via the python -m flag.

Therefore, we can apply the Python profiler to a program file named `program.py` as follows:

```
python -m cProfile program.py
```

This will run the program `program.py` normally. Then once the program is done, profile information will be reported on standard output.

The `cProfile` program takes a number of command line flags.

The -o flag allows us to specify the file in which to store the output of the profiler.

Storing profile results to file is a good practice.

For example:

```
python -m cProfile -o profile.out program.py
```

Note that the data is written in a binary format suitable for the `pstats` module to read and use.

We can provide the -s flag to sort the profile results by one of the table headings.

By default, the profiler results are sorted by cumulative time spent on the function and sub-functions, e.g. `cumtime`.

> **cumtime**: is the cumulative time spent in this and all subfunctions (from invocation till exit). This figure is accurate even for recursive functions.

– The Python Profilers

A common helpful way to sort the results is by the number of calls made to a function, e.g. `ncalls`.

> **ncalls**: for the number of calls.

– The Python Profilers

For example:

```
python -m cProfile -s ncalls program.py
```

This can highlight functions that are called many times and in turn, take a long overall time to execute.

We might also sort the results by the total time spent on each function call, e.g. `tottime`.

> **tottime**: for the total time spent in the given function (and excluding time made in calls to sub-functions)

– The Python Profilers

For example:

```
python -m cProfile -s tottime program.py
```

This can highlight individual function calls that take a long time to run.

Now that we know how to use the Python profiler, let's explore how we might use it to identify slow parts of Python programs.

24.3 Example Of Profiling A Slow Function Call

We can explore using the Python profiler on a program that is slow because it has a long-running function call.

In this example, we will define a function that performs a long blocking call. The function will then be called from the main function.

We will call the `time.sleep()` function which blocks the entire thread, preventing the program from progressing.

```
# long running task
def work():
    # block the thread for a long time
    time.sleep(5)
```

Tying this together, the complete example is listed below.

```
# SuperFastPython.com
# example of a program that has a slow function call
import time

# long running task
def work():
    # block the thread for a long time
    time.sleep(5)

# main program
def main():
    # report a message
    print('Main is running')
    # run our task
    work()
    # report a message
    print('Main is done.')

# protect the entry point
if __name__ == '__main__':
    # start the program
    main()
```

Running the program calls the main() function.

The main() function runs and reports a start message then calls the work() function.

The work() function runs and blocks the main thread with a call to time.sleep() for 5 seconds.

The work() function resumes and terminates.

The `main()` function resumes, reports a final message, and terminates.

```
Main is running
Main is done.
```

Next, we can profile the program, and assume we don't know why the program is slow.

We will use the `cProfile` module and report results with default sorting.

```
python -m cProfile program.py
```

If we are unable to run the `cProfile` program on our system, we can use the `profile` module instead. The results will be identical.

The `cProfile` output reports some details about the program.

For example, there were 8 function calls and the program ran for a little over 5 seconds.

The default output from `cProfile` does not seem helpful in this case, perhaps sorting by cumulative function execution time (`cumtime`) is not the best approach.

Note, the results on your system may differ.

```
Main is running
Main is done.
        8 function calls in 5.005 seconds

Ordered by: cumulative time

   ...cumtime  percall filename:lineno(function)
   ...  5.005    5.005 {built-in method builtins.exec}
   ...  5.005    5.005 program.py:1(<module>)
   ...  5.005    5.005 program.py:11(main)
   ...  5.005    5.005 program.py:6(work)
   ...  5.005    5.005 {built-in method time.sleep}
   ...  0.000    0.000 {built-in method builtins.print}
   ...  0.000    0.000 {...'_lsprof.Profiler' objects}
```

One approach we can try is to filter all results by the name of our program, e.g. `program.py`.

This may give insight into the cumulative execution time of each one of our functions.

A simple way to achieve this is to run the `cProfile` and filter the results for the program name via `grep` on the command line.

For example:

```
python -m cProfile program.py | grep program.py
```

Note that this assumes we have access to the `grep` program on our system. It may not be available on Windows by default.

The results show only the output lines from `cProfile` that mention our program name.

We can see a hierarchy of cumulative time from the top level (or whole program), to the `main()` function on line 11 to our `work()` function on line 6.

Note, the results on your system may differ.

This highlights that the problem is probably somewhere in the `work()` function.

```
1    0.000    0.000    5.001    5.001 program.py:1()
1    0.000    0.000    5.001    5.001 program.py:11(main)
1    0.000    0.000    5.000    5.000 program.py:6(work)
```

Next, let's try sorting the output of `cProfile` by the total execution time of each function, e.g. `tottime`.

```
python -m cProfile -s tottime program.py
```

This helps.

We can see that the first function in the list that has the longest overall execution time is the call to `time.sleep()`.

Note, the results on your system may differ.

This highlights how we can use the output from `cProfile` to zero in on long-running functions in our Python programs.

```
Main is running
Main is done.
    8 function calls in 5.005 seconds


Ordered by: internal time

ncalls  tottime  ... filename:lineno(function)
     1    5.005  ... {built-in method time.sleep}
     2    0.000  ... {built-in method builtins.print}
     1    0.000  ... {built-in method builtins.exec}
     1    0.000  ... program.py:11(main)
     1    0.000  ... program.py:6(work)
     1    0.000  ... program.py:1(<module>)
     1    0.000  ... {'_lsprof.Profiler' objects}
```

Next, let's look at another profiling example, this time with functions that are called many times.

24.4 Example Of Profiling A Repeated Function Call

We can explore using the Python profiler on a program that is slow because it repeatedly makes the same function call.

In this case, we can define a function that performs the same mathematical operation many millions of times, e.g. 100 million calls to `math.sqrt()`

Collectively this is a CPU-bound task and will be slow, but performed in a list comprehension, it does not look like it.

```
# long running task
def work():
```

```
    # block the main thread for a long time
    data = [math.sqrt(i) for i in range(1, 100000000)]
```

Tying this together, the complete example is listed below.

```
# SuperFastPython.com
# example of a program that calls a function repeatedly
import math

# long running task
def work():
    # block the main thread for a long time
    data = [math.sqrt(i) for i in range(1, 100000000)]

# main program
def main():
    # report a message
    print('Main is running')
    # run our task
    work()
    # report a message
    print('Main is done.')

# protect the entry point
if __name__ == '__main__':
    # start the program
    main()
```

Running the program first calls our `main()` function.

The `main()` function runs and reports a start message calls the `work()` function.

The `work()` function runs and executes the list comprehension, creating a list of 100 million square roots of integers.

This takes a while and prevents the main thread from progressing.

Once the list comprehension is complete, the `work()` function terminates.

The `main()` function resumes, reports a final message, and terminates.

```
Main is running
Main is done.
```

Next, let's profile our program and pretend we don't know the cause of why the program is slow.

We can start off by running the `cProfile` with default sorting.

```
python -m cProfile program.py
```

A truncated sample of the output is provided below.

Note, the results on your system may differ.

This does not appear helpful in this case.

It is reporting the internal infrastructure and the first line of our program as having the highest overall cumulative execution time.

```
Main is running
Main is done.
         100000230 function calls in 30.953 seconds

   Ordered by: cumulative time

   ncalls       cumtime       filename:lineno(function)
        1   ... 30.953 ... {built-in builtins.exec}
        1   ... 30.953 ... program.py:1(<module>)
        1   ... 30.952 ... program.py:11(main)
        1   ... 29.840 ... program.py:6(work)
        1   ... 29.840 ... program.py:8(<listcomp>)
 99999999   ...  9.572 ... {built-in method math.sqrt}
   ...
```

Next, let's try sorting results by the total execution time of each function.

```
python -m cProfile -s tottime program.py
```

Here, we can see that line 8 of our program has the highest overall execution time at 20.610 seconds.

This is the line that contains the list comprehension, pointing us in the right direction.

The next function with the largest overall time is `math.sqrt` at 9.611 seconds. Excellent.

Note, the results on your system may differ.

```
Main is running
Main is done.
         100000230 function calls in 31.315 seconds

   Ordered by: internal time

   ncalls  tottime        filename:lineno(function)
        1   20.610   ... program.py:8(<listcomp>)
 99999999    9.611   ... {built-in method math.sqrt}
        1    1.094   ... program.py:11(main)
        1    0.000   ... {built-in method ...}
        5    0.000   ... {built-in method posix.stat}
        2    0.000   ... {built-in method builtins.print}
        1    0.000   ... {built-in method posix.getcwd}
...
```

Let's try another approach.

In this case, let's sort the results by the total number of times each function is called, e.g. `ncalls`.

```
python -m cProfile -s ncalls program.py
```

Now we see some striking results.

We can see that the `math.sqrt` function was called nearly 100 million times, 99,999,999 times to be precise.

This is far and away beyond the calls to any other function and the source of our problem.

```
Main is running
Main is done.
        100000230 function calls in 31.477 seconds

   Ordered by: call count

   ncalls      filename:lineno(function)
 99999999  ... {built-in method math.sqrt}
       32  ... {method 'rstrip' of 'str' objects}
       19  ... <frozen importlib._bootstrap>:244(...)
       16  ... {method 'join' of 'str' objects}
       16  ... <...>:126(_path_join)
       16  ... <...>:128(<listcomp>)
        7  ... {built-in method builtins.getattr}
        6  ... {method 'rpartition' of 'str' objects}
        6  ... {built-in method builtins.hasattr}
        6  ... {built-in method _imp.acquire_lock}
...
```

This highlights how we can zero in on the cause of a problem by reviewing the same profile data in different ways, both execution time and number of function calls.

24.5 Further Reading

This section lists helpful additional resources on the topic.

- Profiling (computer programming), Wikipedia.
  https://w.wiki/7Z8W
- The Python Profilers.
  https://docs.python.org/3/library/profile.html
- `time` – Time access and conversions.
  https://docs.python.org/3/library/time.html
- `math` – Mathematical functions.
  https://docs.python.org/3/library/math.html

24.6 Takeaways

You now know how to profile Python programs in order to discover why they are slow.

Specifically, you know:

- What is code profiling and why it is important.
- How profiling is not benchmarking but an important and related task when optimizing performance.
- How to use the profiler in the standard library to find slow parts of Python code.

24.6.1 Next

In the next tutorial, we will explore how to benchmark using the `time` Unix command.

Chapter 25

Benchmarking With The `time` Command

You can benchmark Python programs without making any modifications to the code by using the `time` command.

In this tutorial, you will discover how to benchmark Python programs using the `time` command.

After completing this tutorial, you will know:

- Why it is important to benchmark a Python program without changing it.
- How to use the `time` Unix command to measure the execution time of a Python program.
- How to interpret the results from the `time` and the benefits and limitations of using it for benchmarking.

Let's get started.

25.1 Need To Benchmark Unobtrusively

Benchmarking Python programs is an essential practice when striving to create efficient, high-performance software.

Most approaches to benchmarking require us to change our programs in order to measure and report the benchmark result. We have seen this with the use of the functions in the `time` module and the custom functions and classes we developed based on those functions.

Nevertheless, sometimes we need to benchmark our entire Python program without making any direct changes to it.

Three reasons we may need to benchmark a Python program without changing it include:

1. To collect non-intrusive measurements
2. To ensure reusability and reproducibility.
3. To ensure consistency and isolation.

Let's take a closer look at each of these concerns in turn.

25.1.1   Non-Intrusive Measurement

One of the key reasons for using a separate benchmarking program is to ensure non-intrusive measurement.

When we add benchmarking code directly into our script, it becomes a part of the script's logic. This not only adds overhead to the measurements but can also alter the behavior of our code, making the results less accurate.

By using a separate benchmarking program, we can measure the script's performance without modifying the code itself, ensuring that our measurements reflect the script's actual execution and are not influenced by the benchmarking process.

25.1.2   Reusability and Reproducibility

Another compelling reason is reusability and reproducibility.

With a dedicated benchmarking program, we can easily measure the performance of multiple scripts without duplicating code. We can create standardized benchmarks that are easily reproducible, making it simpler to compare the performance of different scripts or versions of our code.

This reusability and reproducibility are critical when we're working on projects that involve numerous iterations and continuous performance evaluations.

25.1.3   Consistency and Isolation

A separate benchmarking program also offers the advantage of consistency and isolation.

It ensures that our benchmarking logic and metrics remain consistent across different projects. Moreover, it isolates the benchmarking process from the actual functionality of our script, which is crucial for maintaining a clean and clear codebase.

This separation of concerns allows us to focus on our code's core functionality while still having the ability to analyze its performance independently.

Now that we have seen the need to benchmark Python programs unobtrusively, let's take a closer look at one approach that we can use.

25.2   Benchmark With The `time` Command

The `time` command is a tool that can be used to measure the execution time of any program on the command line interface.

Let's take a closer look at the `time` command.

25.2.1   What Is The `time` Command

Recall that the command line or command line interface is a way of interacting with the computer using text commands, as opposed to clicking around on a graphical interface with a mouse.

The `time` command, also called the `time` Unix command, is a command line program for reporting the execution time of programs.

> In computing, time is a command in Unix and Unix-like operating systems. It is used to determine the duration of execution of a particular command.

– time (Unix), Wikipedia.

It is referred to as the "`time` Unix command" because it was originally developed for the Unix operating system.

The command is available on almost all Unix-like operating systems and may be implemented as an executable command (e.g. GNU time) or as a keyword in the shell (e.g. bash time).

Recall that we can execute a Python program directly using the Python interpreter. This can be achieved by specifying the `python` command followed by the program name.

The `time` command runs a program, such as a Python program, and reports the overall execution time.

This approach is recommended if we want to benchmark the entire program without modifying it anyway.

It returns 3 benchmark results, real-time, user time, and system time.

Real-time is the wall clock time, the duration of the program. The CPU time is calculated as the sum of user time and system time which specify how long the program spent in each mode.

If the program is blocked by other programs running at the same time or sleeps, the CPU time may be shorter than the real-time. This is because clocks that record CPU time are paused when the program is blocked, and resume once the program resumes executing.

- **Real-time**: Wall-clock execution time of the program.
- **CPU-time**: Sum of user time and system time when executing the program.

- **User-time**: Time the CPU spent executing user code (our program and dependencies).
- **System-time**: Time the CPU spent executing in the kernel (operating system).

Next, let's consider the benefits of the `time` command.

25.2.2 Benefits Of The `time` Command

Using the `time` Unix command to benchmark Python code provides several benefits, especially when we need a quick and simple way to measure the overall execution time of a program.

Below are some advantages of using the `time` command for benchmarking:

1. **Quick and Convenient**: The `time` command is readily available on Unix-like systems, making it a convenient option for quickly measuring the execution time of a Python program without the need for additional code modifications.
2. **No Code Modification**: We don't need to modify our Python code to perform benchmarking. Simply prefix the Python command with the `time` command in the terminal.
3. **Total Execution Time**: The `time` command provides the total wall-clock time taken by the Python program to complete its execution, including any setup and teardown operations.
4. **Simple Output**: The output of the `time` command provides information about real (wall clock), user, and system time, which can give us insights into the distribution of time spent during execution.
5. **Measures All Overheads**: The `time` command measures all overheads associated with the execution of the Python program, including interpreter startup, module loading, and other setup operations.

Despite these benefits, it's important to note that the `time` command has limitations.

25.2.3   Limitations Of The `time` Command

The `time` command is not available on all platforms.

Generally, it is available on Unix and Unix-like systems, such as Linux and macOS.

It is not available on Windows platforms by default.

Nevertheless, it can be installed using a third-party software package, such as Cygwin or Microsoft PowerToys.

25.3   How To Benchmark With The `time` Command

The `time` command is used by pre-pending it to a normal command on the command line.

When using `time` to benchmark the execution time of Python programs, it is prepended to the `python` command.

For example:

```
time python myprogram.py
```

This will run the Python program normally.

Once the program is completed, a summary of the execution time will be reported.

And that's all there is to it.

25.4   Example Of Benchmarking With The `time` Command

We can explore how to benchmark a Python program using the `time` command.

In this case, we can develop our program normally. We do not need to modify it to add any benchmarking code.

Our program will call a function that performs some CPU-intensive task. It will create a list of 100 million squared integers.

The complete program is listed below.

```
# SuperFastPython.com
# example of a python program that can be benchmarked

# function to benchmark
def task():
    # create a large list
    data = [i*i for i in range(100000000)]

# protect the entry point
if __name__ == '__main__':
    # run the task
    task()
```

We can then save our program to a file, such as **benchmark_time.py**.

Normally we would execute the program from the command line using the python command.

For example:

```
python benchmark_time.py
```

In order to benchmark the execution time of the Python program, we can prepend the **time** command to the execution of our program.

For example:

```
time python benchmark_time.py
```

Running the example reports the execution time both in terms of real-time (wall clock time) and CPU time (user + sys).

I recommend focusing on the reported real-time.

In this case, we can see that the program took about 6.335 seconds to complete.

Note, the results on your system may differ.

This highlights how we can benchmark a Python program using the `time` command.

```
real    0m6.335s
user    0m5.169s
sys     0m1.133s
```

25.5 Further Reading

This section lists helpful additional resources on the topic.

- Benchmarking, Wikipedia.
  https://en.wikipedia.org/wiki/Benchmarking
- Command-line interface, Wikipedia.
  https://en.wikipedia.org/wiki/Command-line_interface
- time (Unix), Wikipedia.
  https://en.wikipedia.org/wiki/Time_(Unix)
- GNU time.
  https://www.gnu.org/software/time/
- Cygwin.
  https://cygwin.com/
- Microsoft PowerToys.
  https://learn.microsoft.com/en-us/windows/powertoys/

25.6 Takeaways

You now know how to benchmark Python programs using the `time` command.

Specifically, you know:

- Why it is important to benchmark a Python program without changing it.
- How to use the `time` Unix command to measure the execution time of a Python program.
- How to interpret the results from the `time` and the benefits and limitations of using it for benchmarking.

25.6.1   Next

This was the last tutorial, next we will look back at how far you have come.

Conclusions

Chapter 26

Conclusions

26.1 Look Back At How Far You've Come

Congratulations, you made it to the end.

Let's take a look back and review what you now know.

1. You know how to use functions from the `time` module for benchmarking, including:

1. How to benchmark statements, functions, and programs using the 5 functions for measuring time in the `time` module.
2. How to know when and why to use functions like `time.perf_counter()` and `time.monotonic()` over `time.time()`.
3. How to know when and why to use functions like `time.thread_time()` and `time.process_time()`.

2. You know benchmarking best practices and when to use them, including:

1. How to calculate and report benchmark results in terms of difference and speedup.

2. How to and why to repeat benchmark tests and report summary statistics like the average.
3. How to consider the precision and units of measure of reported benchmark results.

3. You know how to develop convenient benchmarking tools, including:

1. How to develop a custom benchmarking helper function and stopwatch class.
2. How to develop a custom benchmarking context manager.
3. How to develop a custom benchmarking function decorator.

4. You know how to benchmark asyncio programs and develop convenient async-specific benchmarking tools, including:

1. How to benchmark asyncio programs using the event loop timer.
2. How to develop a custom benchmarking coroutine.
3. How to develop a custom benchmarking asynchronous context manager and coroutine decorator.

5. You know how to benchmark snippets using the `timeit` module, including:

1. How to benchmark statements and functions using the `timeit` Python API.
2. How to benchmark snippets of code using the `timeit` command line interface.

6. You know how to use other benchmarking tools, including:

1. How to profile Python programs with the built-in profiler and know the relationship between benchmarking and profiling.
2. How to benchmark the execution time of Python programs unobtrusively using the `time` Unix command.

Thank you for letting me help you on your journey into Python concurrency.

Jason Brownlee, Ph.D.
SuperFastPython.com
2023.

26.2 Resources For Diving Deeper

This section lists some useful additional resources for further reading.

- High Performance Python, Ian Ozsvald, et al., 2020.
  https://amzn.to/3wRD5MX
- Python Concurrency with asyncio, Matt Fowler, 2022.
  https://amzn.to/3LZvxNn
- Effective Python, Brett Slatkin, 2019.
  https://amzn.to/3GpopJ1
- Python Cookbook, David Beazley, et al., 2013.
  https://amzn.to/3MSFzBv
- Python in a Nutshell, Alex Martelli, et al., 2017.
  https://amzn.to/3m7SLGD

26.3 Getting More Help

Do you have any questions?

Below provides some great places online where you can ask questions about Python programming and Python concurrency:

- Stack Overview.
  https://stackoverflow.com/
- Python Subreddit.
  https://www.reddit.com/r/python
- LinkedIn Python Developers Community.
  https://www.linkedin.com/groups/25827
- Quora Python (programming language).
  https://www.quora.com/topic/Python-programming-language-1

26.3.1   Contact the Author

You are not alone.

If you ever have any questions about the tutorials in this book, please contact me directly:

- Jason@SuperFastPython.com

I will do my best to help.

About the Author

Jason Brownlee, Ph.D. helps Python developers bring modern concurrency methods to their projects with hands-on tutorials. Learn more at SuperFastPython.com.

Jason is a software engineer and research scientist with a background in artificial intelligence and high-performance computing. He has authored more than 20 technical books on machine learning and has built, operated, and exited online businesses.

Figure 26.1: Photo of Jason Brownlee

www.ingramcontent.com/pod-product-compliance
Lightning Source LLC
LaVergne TN
LVHW051427050326
832903LV00030BD/2951